KOBE B| THE BLACK MAMBA

History, Anecdotes, Famous Phrases and Analysis of the Black Mamba Mentality

Gregg Thompson

...in loving memory of Kobe and Gigi Bryant

TABLE OF CONTENTS

INTRODUCTION

Kobe Bryant took more attempts than any other star—and that is what made this living legend special to him, who earned five NBA titles and two Olympic gold medals and who was the all-time Los Angeles Lakers achieved under his new youth trainer law. Instead, it indicated that he had the same attitude that he had with the Lakers' titles with his new position. Whether you were a teammate in the Hall of Fame or a young dance enthusiast didn't matter; Bryant would ask for you the most.

He named it the mindset of Mamba and wrote a book. "I liked to challenge and to make them uncomfortable," he wrote in an extract published on the Tribune of the Players. "This leads to introspection, and this leads to improvement. One might tell I encouraged people to be their brightest. "It was not a characteristic that contributed to a celebrity rivalry; it was a notoriously tricky competitor during his years. His former head coach Phil Jackson once wrote a book in which Bryant was called "uncoachable." Bryant didn't argue the point correctly.

Bryant was the son of Joe Bryant, a retired NBA player. He attended high school Lower Merion in Pennsylvania, known as the country's top high school basketball player. Upon college, he entered the NBA

Draft for 1996 and was chosen to take the 13th overall selection by Charlotte Hornets; instead, the Hornets transferred him to the Lakers. Bryant won himself a reputation as a high-flyer and a fan by capturing the Slam Dunk Contest in 1997 and by his second season he was named an All-Star. The duo led the Lakers to three straight NBA titles from 2000 to 2002 following feuds with friend Shaquille O'Neal. In 2003, a 19-year-old hotel clerk accused Bryant of sexual assault. Criminal charges were brought and later dropped after the defendant refused to testify, and the criminal case was eventually settled out of court. Bryant denied the command of the attack but confessed to a romantic occurrence and made public apologies. But these charges found his public profile to have been harmed, which resulted in the loss of many sponsorships.

After the Lakers missed the 2004 NBA Finals, Bryant became the central figure for the Lakers. In the 2005–06 and 2006–07 seasons, he guided the NBA. In 2006, he recorded 81 points in his career, the second-highest goals in a single match in the League's history after Wilt Chamberlain's 100-point game of 1962. Between 2009 and 2010, Bryant led the team to two straight titles and, on both times, earned the NBA Finals MVP. He stayed among the leading League players until 2013 when he sustained a torn Achilles tendon at 34. While he improved from the accident, he sustained constant knee and shoulder injuries in the ensuing two seasons. Bryant retired after the 2015–16 season, noting his physical decline.

Bryant was 34 years old and 104 days old, the youngest player in the league's history to hit 30,000 career points. On 1 February 2010, he was the leading scorer in Lakers ' franchise history, passing Jerry West. Bryant was also the first player to play at least 20 seasons in NBA history. The 18 All-Star designations are the second most often, while they are the record number one starting point for most straight appearances. For most of NBA history, Bryant's four All-Star MVP Awards are related to Bob Pettit. In the mid-2000s, he called himself "Black Mamba," and the general public has widely adopted the epithet. He earned two gold medals as a part of the U.S. national team at the 2008 and 2012 Summer Olympics. In 2018, he won the Best Animated Short Film academy award for his 2017 Dear Basketball script.

On 26 January 2020, Bryant and his 13-year-old daughter Gianna and seven others were killed in a Calabasas, California helicopter crash.

But he was phenomenally successful, as he overexposed his critics worse than he expected when you were on the same hand. Bryant would be the first to admit why he saw Michael Jordan as every NBA player of his generation did. He brought Jordan's famed competitive nature to its logical endpoint in his playing style. Where Jordan concealed his society behind a flat, brilliant person created by Madison Avenue, Bryant took the opposite path and played the game, practically fueled by boos. If you found yourself a poisonous serpent, you knew you would not be the laughing star of a film by Warner Bros. Bryant wrote in the Mamba Mentality, "I just wanted to kill the resistance.

Let's not ignore that he first took on the Black Mamba name. When the Kent Babb of the Washington Post paraphrased the shooting guard in a shocking article, Bryant thought that performing this role was "the only way it could go beyond the events of Colorado." In reality, these "idents" lead to a sexual assault charge in 2003 and subsequent trial. After the defendant refused to testify, the criminal case against him was dropped, and a civil suit was decided afterward. After the appeal, Bryant's comments were dismissed, "I can appreciate how she thought she didn't accept this experience." Robert Silverman of the Daily Beast firmly suggested that Bryant also used the reality that a significant portion of the population considered it an abuser as his motivation was on the bench. In an all-too-common sports tale, a story of violence against women started to be slowly re-written in a narrative about competitor overcoming adversity.

In the end, Bryant was paying off with the plan. Throughout the rest of his career, Bryant remained willing to be a one-person team on the field, a bucket terminator. Bryant's version recorded 81 points during a 2006 contest, the second-highest number in NBA history, against the Toronto Raptors. It was this Bryant who won his last two titles without the tremendous influence of Shaq. When the League became profoundly concerned with shot efficiency at the end of his career, Bryant also fiercely rebelled against the period's shifting intellect. He would become famous for his broad nights of shooting, taking and often make low-value shots at a pace almost counterproductive to basic mathematical principles. It was very appropriate for him to score 60 points in his last NBA game in an impressive 50 shot attempt.

WHO IS KOBE BRYANT?

Kobe Bryant lived his early years in Italy and straight from high school entered the NBA. Dominant scorer, Bryant earned five NBA titles and the Los Angeles Lakers MVP Award in 2008. While injuries were incurred later in the seasons, Michael Jordan finished in December 2014 for third on the NBA all-time scoring chart and retired in 2016 after score 60 points in his final game. In 2018, Bryant won the Dear Basketball Academy Award for Best Animated Short Movie. On January 26, 2020, Bryant, his 13-year-old daughter Gigi, and seven others were involved in a helicopter crash.

Early Life

Kobe Bean Bryant was born in Philadelphia, Pennsylvania, on 23 August 1978. The son of ex-NBA player Joe "Jellybean" Bryant was named after a city in Japan.

Following his NBA career in 1984, Bryant's elder took his family to Italy and starred in the Italian League. Bryant was an avid player in basketball and soccer, growing up in Italy and two competitive older sisters, Shaya and Sharia. When the family moved to Philadelphia in 1991, Bryant represented the Lower Merion High

School basketball team for four years. With an emphasis on the NBA, he even began to work with the 76.

Bryant, the eldest of three daughters, and the only son of former NBA player Joe Bryant and Pamela Cox Bryant, was raised in Philadelphia. He was the maternal nephew of John "Chubby" Cox, the basketball player. After Kobe, his parents named him Japan's famous beef, which they saw on the restaurant menu[9]. His middle name Bean was taken from his father's' Jellybean' nickname. The father of Bryant was Protestant, and he had upheld his religion often.

At the age of three, Bryant started playing hoops, and the Lakers became his favorite team as he grew up. At the age of six, Bryant graduated from the NBA and moved his family to Rieti, Italy, to continue to play professional basketball on a lower level. We transferred to Reggio Calabria for two years, then to Pistoia and Reggio Emilia. Kobe grew used to his new lifestyle and learned to speak Italian fluently. He particularly loved Reggio Emilia, a place of affection and where some of his youth's best memories were made. Bryant seriously started playing basketball while staying in Reggio Emilia. The grandparents of Bryant will give Bryant recordings of NBA games to review. He also learned to play football, and his favorite football team was A.C. Milan. Milan. Every college, Bryant will travel to the USA and participate in a professional basketball league. He and his father relocated to Philadelphia at the age of thirteen.

High school

Bryant has gained national recognition through his stellar high school career in the Lower Merion High School in Ardmore in the Lower Merion neighborhood of Philadelphia. He played as a freshman on the varsity basketball team. Bryant became the first rookie for the Lower Merion varsity team in several decades, but the team finished with 4-20. The Aces built 77–13 results in three years, with Bryant playing all five positions. In his junior year, he scored 31.1 points, 10.4 rebounds, and 5.2 assists and was named Pennsylvania Player of the Year and received a fourth-team All-American Parade award draw from college recruiters. His best rankings featured Stanford, Florida, North Carolina, and Villanova. When Kevin Garnett went to secondary school in the first round of the 1995 draft NBA, Bryant still started to think about going directly to the majors.

Bryant received the 1995 Senior MVP Award at Nike ABCD Camp with former NBA colleague Lamar Odom. In high school, then 76-strong coach John

Lucas allowed Bryant to work out and scrap the band, along alongside Jerry Stackhouse, one-on-one. During his high school senior year, Bryant guided the Aces during 53 years to their first state championship. He posted 30.8 points, 12 blocks, 6.5 assists, four steals, and 3.8 blocked shots to a 31-3 record for Aces in the stretch. Bryant completed his high school career at 2 883 points as the all-time leading scorer in Southeastern Pennsylvania, outperforming Wilt Chamberlain and Lionel Simmons.

Bryant was given many honors for his excellent performance at the Lower Merion during his senior year. These include Naismith High School Year Champion, Gatorade Men's National Basketball Player of the Year, McDonald's All-America, the first All-American Parade Team, and the USA Today All-USA First Team Player. Greg Downer, the varsity coach of Bryant, said that he is "a complete player who wins" and lauded his work ethic as the team's top athlete. Bryant introduced R&B star Brandy to his high school in 1996. As a result, Bryant, a 17-year-old, decided to go straight into the League and became the sixth player in NBA history. Bryant's announcement was very well handled at a moment of rare ready-to-use NBA players (Garnett being the only exception in 20 years). His basketball skills and 1080 SAT score would have meant that he would be accepted into any university, but he did not officially visit any campus. Bryant was named as one of the 35 top McDonald's Americans in 2012.

While Bryant enjoyed good grades and strong SAT scores, he opted to go from high school straight to the NBA. He was drafted by the Charlotte Hornets and dealt with the Los Angeles Lakers with the 13th overall selection from the 1996 NBA draft.

NBA Career and Stats

Bryant was elected a first for the 1998 All-Star Game in his second season with the Lakers, rendering him the youngest All-Star in the NBA history at 19 years. The shooting guard later played with the Superstar Center Shaquille O'Neal for three straight NBA Championships, and from 2002-2004 they were named first-team all-NBA. He has also entered into multi-year deals with Nike, Sprite, and other significant partners.

1996 NBA draft

Before the NBA draft for 1996, Bryant had been practicing in Los Angeles, where he went up fellow Lakers stars Larry Drew and Michael Cooper, who "was marching over these guys," according to then-Laker boss Jerry West.

The Lakers agreed to swap their Vlade Divac starting center for player draft rights and free up salary caps so that they could sell the Shaquille O'Neal free-fire core. At that moment, Bill Branch, the head agent of Charlotte Hornets, informed Lakers that the Hornets agreed to trade their draft selection around #13 the day before the draft. The Hornets never acknowledged Bryant's drafting before the trade agreement. The Lakers informed the Hornets during the lottery to choose minutes before the selection was completed. Bryant was the first guard recruited from high school directly. After the pick, the exchange was jeopardized by Divac's decision to withdraw instead of selling from Los Angeles.

Nevertheless, on 30 June, Divac relented on its demand and concluded the deal on 9 July 1996, when the ban on the off-season League expired. His parents had to consign an agreement with the Lakers, as Bryant was 17 when he was 18 before the season started until he signed his contract. Bryant has agreed to a $3.5 million rookie contract spanning three years.

Adjusting to the NBA (1996–1999)

Bryant made his debut at the Long Beach, California Summer Pro League and recorded 25 points ahead of a standing room only audience. Defenders fought hard to get in front of him, and West and Lakers coach Del Harris was enthusiastic about his success. He recorded 36 points in the final and ended in four games with 24.5 points and 5.3 rebounds. Bryant was primarily murdered as a novice in 1996-1997 behind the guards Eddie Jones and Nick Van Exel. He was the youngest player to ever play in an NBA game (18 years, 72 days) and was also the youngest NBA starter (18 years and 158 days), a mark held by Jermaine O'Neal and former team-mate Andrew Bynum. Initially, Bryant appeared for a few minutes, but he started to see some more action as the season continues.

He played 15.5 minutes per game by the end of the season. Bryant took part in the Rookie Showdown during the All-Star weekend and captured the 1997 Slam Dunk Contest, which became the youngest dunk winner at 18. Bryant has maintained his success throughout the year with his reserve player Travis Knight on the NBA All-Rookie Second Team.

The Lakers progressed to the Western Conference's semi-finals until Bryant was moved to a leading role at the end of Game 5. Byron Scott missed the game with a sprained wrist, Robert Horry was suspended for fighting against Jeff Hornacek of Utah, and Shaquille O'Neal was out in the fourth quarter with 1:46 remaining. At the end of the game, Bryant fired four airballs; the Jazz took overtime 98–93 to defeat the Lakers 4-1. He first hit a two-point hop in the fourth quarter and then misfired three overtime three-point field goals, two of them tied in the final minute. Bryant] was the only one who had the guts at the moment to take these attempts," elaborated O'Neal. "He had more time in the second season of Bryant and started showing more of his talents as a talented young player. This has more than doubled Bryant's point total, from 7.6 to 15.4 points per game. Bryant would have seen a rise in minutes when the Lakers were "acting huge," with Bryant typically playing tiny with the guards. Bryant was the recipient of the NBA's Sixth Man of the Year Award and became the youngest NBA All-Star player in the NBA's history with fan voting. Teammates O'Neal, Van Exel and Jones accompanied him, and it was the first time since 1983 that four players from the same roster were picked for the same All-Star Game. The best of any non-starter in this season, Bryant's 15.4 points per game.

The 1998-99 season marked the rise of Bryant as the pioneer in the game. Traded with Van Exel and Jones starting guards, Bryant began every game during the 50-game lockout season. During the season, Bryant signed a six-year $70 million contract. He stayed with the Lakers until the conclusion of the 2003-04 season. Sportswriters contrasted his talents with Michael Jordan and Magic Johnson at an early stage of his career. Nonetheless, the postseason outcomes were no more reliable because the Lakers were defeated by the San Antonio Spurs in the Western Semifinals conference.

Although the Lakers battled for O'Neal's exit in 2004, Bryant played beautifully. In January of this year, he posted 81 points against the Toronto Raptors, the second-highest single-game in NBA history.

In 2008 Bryant was named the Boston Celtics ' Most Valuable Player and took his side to the NBA Finals. The Lakers defeated the Orlando Magic in the 2009 NBA Finals to win the championship. Soon after that, Bryant became part of Michael Jackson's memorial service to remember buddy and pioneer of rock. The next year, they won their second consecutive championship by beating the Celtics.

Bryant appeared in the United States between 2008 and 2012. Olympic teams are winning successive gold medals amongst other top players, including Kevin Durant, LeBron James, and Carmelo Anthony.

Three-peat (1999–2002)

As Phil Jackson took office in 1999 as president of the Lakers, Bryant's prospects will change. With years of continuous development, Bryant became one of League's top shooting guards, taking part in the All-NBA, All-Star, and All-Defensive teams in the league. The Lakers were championed under Bryant and O'Neal, who created a great mix of center guards. Jackson used the triangle offense he was using with the Chicago Bulls to earn six titles, which would see both Bryant and O'Neal ascend to the NBA elite class. There were three successive tournaments in 2000, 2001 and 2002 that further reinforced this belief.

Bryant was set aside for six weeks before the 1999-2000 season because of a hand injury he had sustained in a pre-season match against the Wizards in Washington. As Bryant came back and played a game for more than 38 minutes, all the statistical metrics improved in the 1999-2000 season. This included leading the team to support every game and to rob every game. With a stable fund, the O'Neal and Bryant pair won the Lakers 67 games, tied to the fifth largest in the NBA history. It coincided with O'Neal being voted MVP and Bryant for the first time in his career (the youngest player to win defensive awards) in the prestigious Third and All-NBA Defensive

Prestigious of All-NBA. During O'Neal's second playoff game, Bryant performed a 25-point, 11-point recovery, seven-play, and4-block performance in Appearance 7 of the western conference finals against the Portland Trail Blazers. He tossed an O'Neal alley-oop pass to catch the game and the series. In the 2000 Playoffs, Bryant injured his ankle on the foot of the Pacers ' Jalen Rose in the second quarter of game 2. Rose later admitted that he intentionally placed his foot under Bryant. Bryant didn't come back to the team, so he missed Game 3 because of the injury. In Game 4, Bryant tallied 22 points in the second half, which helped O'Neal win. Bryant took the shot to put the Lakers 120-118 ahead. The Lakers captured their first title since 1988 with a 116-111 Game 6 victory.

Statistically, Bryant spent the same year in the 2000–01 season as the previous year but scored six more per game (28.5). It was also the year that Bryant and O'Neal started to dispute. Bryant again led the team, with five per game. The Lakers played just 56 games, a drop-off of 11 from last year. The Lakers will respond in the playoffs 15-1. In the first round, they quickly swept the Portland Trail Blazers. The Lakers defeated the Sacramento Kings in the playoffs. In-Game 4 against the Kings, Bryant has won 119–113 rebounds with 48 points, 16 rebounds, and three assists. They routed the San Antonio Spurs into the conference's final when they dropped their first match in overtime against the Philadelphian 76ers. We will take the next four games in as many seasons to deliver a second championship to Los Angeles. Bryant also played heavy minutes in the playoffs, making his numbers up to 29.4 points, 7.3 rebounds, and 6.1 assists per game. Teammate O'Neal proclaimed Bryant to be the best player in the league in the postseason. Bryant completed the second year in a row as the All NBA Second Team and the All NBA Defensive Team. He was also named for the third consecutive year of the NBA All-Star Game (no game in 1999).

In 2001-02 for the first time in his career, Bryant started 80 minutes. On 14 January 2002, Bryant recorded a 56-point career, accompanied by five rebounds and four assists in a 120-81 victory over Memphis Grizzlies. He continued his entire game by a total of 25.2 points, 5.5 assists, and 5.5 bits of help per session. Bryant also had a 46.9% overall shot and led his team once again. After a 31-point effort in Philadelphia, he won his first All-Star MVP award as a fan of the game, arising from his earlier advice to a 76ers heckler during the finals that the lakers wanted "to cut your hearts off." Bryant was also selected to the All-NBA First Team for the first time in his career as he also made the All-NBA Defensive team. The Lakers played 58 games the same year and finished second to state competitor Sacramento Kings in the Pacific Division. Bryant was suspended one game after he struck Reggie Miller from the Pacers after the Pacers victory at Lakers on 1 March 2002.

The journey to the Finals will be even more accessible than the Laker's success the previous year had achieved. While in the first two rounds of the playoffs, the Lakers hurled the Blazers and beat the Spurs 4–1, the Lakers had no home-court advantage over the Sacramento Kings. The series will run to seven rounds, first since the 2000 Western Conference Finals in Lakers. The Lakers were able to battle their opponents and take part in their third consecutive NBA Finals. During the 2002 Playoffs, Bryant scored 26.8 points, 51.4% accuracy, 5.8 blocks, 5.3 assists per game, and a fifth of its goals. Bryant was the first player to win three titles at 23 years of age. His performance in the fourth quarter, particularly the last two rounds of playoffs, was remarkable and lauded. Bryant's status as a "clutch player" was cemented.

Coming up short (2002–2004)

In the first game of the 2002–03 season, Bryant had 27 points, ten assists, five bits of help, and four thefts for the hosting Spurs during an 87–82 defeat. In a 108–93 victory over LA Clippers on November 1, Bryant registered three times as many as 33 points, 15 rebounds, and 12 assists. He also set a three-pointer

NBA mark in a game on 7 January 2003 when he scored twelve against the Seattle SuperSonics. Bryant averaged 30 points per game and took a historic run, posting 40 or more points in nine consecutive games and averaging 40.6 points throughout the whole month of February.

Furthermore, he averages 6.9 rebounds, 5.9 assists, and 2.2 steals per game. Once again, Bryant was named first for both the All-NBA and All-Defensive teams and sixth in the MVP award. After 50–32, they floundered in the plays and lost to the eventual NBA champion San Antonio Spurs in the Western Conference semi-finals in six games.

League All-Stars might be picked up by Karl Malone and Gary Payton in the next season to drive the NBA championship. Bryant was charged before the season for sexual assault. This led Bryant to miss certain games because of court appeals or come to court earlier to play games later that day. The Lakers played the Portland Trail Blazers in the final game of the regular season. Bryant made two buzzer-beaters for the tournament and the championship of the Pacific Division. Bryant did a three-pointer at the end of the fourth quarter, with 1,1 seconds remaining to send it into overtime. The game eventually moved on to a second overtime, with Bryant taking the time to bring the Lakers over Blazer, 105–104, another three-pointer.

The Lakers were able to reach the NBA Finals with a starting line-up of O'Neal, Malone, Payton, and Bryant. Nevertheless, the Detroit Pistons, who have won their first title since 1990, were beaten in five days. Bryant averaged 22.6 points per game in this series and 4.4 supports. He fired 35.1% of the floor. The contract of Jackson as a coach has not been renewed, and Rudy Tomyanovich has taken over. For Lamar Odom, Caron Butler, and Brian Grant, O'Neal was traded to the Miami Heat. On the following day, Bryant refused to sign an offer for seven years with the Los Angeles Clippers and re-signed it with the Lakers.

Scoring records and playoff upsets (2004–2007)

During the 2004–05 season, Bryant was carefully examined and blamed for his image badly damaged from everything in the previous year. The last season, a family in pursuit of his identity, Jackson penned a particularly damaging salvo. The book describes the Lakers ' chaotic 2003–04 season circumstances and criticizes Bryant in several ways. Jackson named Bryant "uncoachable" in his journal. In the mid-season, Tomjanovich abruptly retired as a coach for Lakers, blaming chronic health problems and fatigue. The remainder of the Lakers ' season was handled without Tomjanovich by former assistant coach Frank Hamblen. Bryant was the second-leading scorer of the Nba, with 27.6 points per match but was surrounded by a cast, and the Lakers were 34-48, and for the first time in more than a decade, the playoffs had been avoided. This year meant a decline in Bryant's overall standing in the NBA, as he did not make the NBA All-Defensive Team. Bryant also engaged in public feuds with Malone and Ray Allen during the season.

In the 2005-2006 season, Bryant's basketball career was at a crossroads. Despite previous disagreements with Bryant, Jackson came back to train the Lakers. Bryant embraced the move, and the two men worked together for the second time in all roles and guided the Lakers back into the playoffs. The individual achievements in Bryant's performance contributed to the best statistical season of his career. On the 20th December 2005, Bryant recorded 62 points against the Dallas Mavericks in three parts. In the fourth quarter, Bryant scored the entire Mavericks team 62–61, the only time that a player did this three-quarter since the shot clock introduction. On the 16th January 2006, when The Lakers played the Miami Heat, Bryant and Shaquille O'Neal took to the news with handshakes and kisses before the game that signaled a turnaround in the rivalry between them. A month later, the two were seen joking together at the 2006 NBA All-Star Game.

Bryant posted a career-high 81 points on January 22, 2006, in a 122–104 victory over the Toronto Raptors. In addition to breaking Elgin Baylor's previous franchise record of 71, Bryant's 81-point game was NBA's second-highest point in history and was only surpassed in the 100-point game of Chamberlain in 1962. Although Chamberlain has frequently been powered by teammates for blow-out shots inside, Bryant has provided his chance, mostly from the outside, in a game that the Lakers have followed by 14 and haven't pulled away until the fourth quarter. As his players played better and his performance was more prolific, Chamberlain recorded 59% of Philadelphia's 169-147 winning points, contrasted with Bryant, who produced 66% of the Lakers ' 122 points. In the same month, Bryant became the first player to score 45 points or more during four consecutive games since 1964, and the only others to do so were Chamberlain and Baylor. Bryant scored 43.4 points per game in January, the eight best months in NBA history and the highest for all non-Chamberlain teams. By the end of the 2005-06 season, Bryant had registered Lakers ' one-season franchise for more than 40 points (27) and scored most points (2832). For the first time, he won the league's leading award by an average of 35.4 points per game, being only the fifth player in league history to score 35 a season. Bryant finished fourth in the 2006 NBA Most Valuable Player

Award but received 22 votes first— second only to Steve Nash.

Later in the season, Bryant's uniform number was changed from 8 to 24 at the outset of the 2006-07 season. The first high school number of Bryant was 24 before he switched to 33. After the Lakers season came to an end, Bryant told TNT he needed 24 rookies, but it was, like 33, impossible; he retired with Kareem Abdul-Jabbar. Bryant had 143 in Adidas ABCD camp and had 8 of them added. The Lakers performed well enough in the first playoff round to gain a 3-1 advantage over the Phoenix Suns, which resulted in Bryant's overtime pushing and winning shot at Game 4. They come within six seconds of removing the Suns in Game 6, but they fell 126–118 in overtime. While Bryant's 27.9 points per series game, the Lakers folded and eventually fell to the Suns in seven games. After scoring 50 points on 20 of 35 Game 6 shoots, Bryant was reported only to have taken three shots in the second half of the 121–90 Game 7 loss to Phoenix.

During the 2006-07 season, Bryant was chosen to play his ninth All-Star Game appearance, and he earned the second All-Star Game MVP trophy on February 18, with 31 points, six assists, and six robberies. During the season, Bryant participated in many incidents in court. On 28 January, trying to get in contact with a potential game-winning jump shot, he shot his arm and hit Manu Ginóbili's defender, San Antonio Spurs, in front of his elbow. After a league investigation, Bryant was banned from the New York Knicks for the Madison Square Garden tie. The justification of the punishment was that Bryant made an "unnatural gesture" by throwing his arm backward. He then seemed to replicate the gesture on 6 March, this time hitting Marko Jarić, guard of Minnesota Timberwolves. The NBA gave a second one-game suspension to Bryant on March 7. In his first match on 9 March, he bowed Kyle Korver in the nose, retroactively re-classified as a flagrant Type 1.

On the 16th of March, Bryant recorded 65 points in a home match against the Portland Trail Blazers that put a 7-game defeat run to a close. This was the second-best outcome of his 11-year career. In the next game, Bryant posted 50 points against Minnesota Timberwolves, after which he recorded 60 points in the road win against the Memphis Grizzlies— the second to record three consecutive more games with more than 50 points, an accomplishment that Jordan has not seen since 1987. The only other Laker was Baylor, who in December 1962 still achieved 50+ in 3 straight competitions. In a match against New Orleans / Oklahoma City Hornets the next day, Bryant recorded 50 points and became NBA's second player to have four consecutive 50-point games after Chamberlain, who was twice hit with a set of five-seven. Bryant ended the year with a record of ten more than 50 points, overtaken by Chamberlain only. Bryant won his second consecutive score award that season as well. During the season 2006-07, his mailbox was the top-selling NBA jersey in the US and China. Some newspapers linked Bryant's new number to increased revenue and his continued All-Star success. In the 2007 NBA playoffs, the Lakers were again defeated by Phoenix Suns, 4-1 in the first round.

Back on top (2007–2010)

On 27 May 2007, ESPN confirmed that Bryant said he wanted to be traded if Jerry West did not return to the full-service team. Bryant later confirmed his wish for West's return to the franchise but denied stating that he would like to be traded if it did not happen. Nonetheless, on the radio program of Stephen A. Smith, three days later, Bryant expressed anger about the "insider" of Lakers that believed that Bryant was liable for the team's exit from Shaquille O'Neal and publically said that he would like to be traded. Three hours later, Bryant said in another interview that he had rethought his assertion after he had spoken to coach Jackson. On 23 December 2007, Bryant · became the youngest player (29 years 122 days) to hit 20,000 points in a game against the New York Knicks, in Madison Square Garden, after recording 39 points with 11 rebounds and eight aids. Bryant had been shown in the notorious Amateur Clip, claiming that the center Andrew Bynum should have been exchanged for all-star Jason Kidd. LeBron James has since surpassed this record. On 28 March, Bryant led the Memphis Grizzlies with a season-high 53 points to fail ten rebounds.

Despite injuries to the small finger of his shooting hand, described as a "complete breaking of the collateral ligament, the airborne fracture and the flying plate accident of the MCP joint," Bryant played all 82 games of the regular season, in the game on 5 February 2008, instead of choosing for surgery. For his injury, he said, "I'd like to postpone some surgery until after our Lakers season and the Olympic Games this summer. But it's an injury that I[sic] and the medical personnel of Lakers will have to continue to watch daily."

Helped by the All-Star Pau Gasol family, Bryant led his team to a West-leading record of 57-25. The Lakers defeated the Nuggets in the first round and on May 6, 2008. Bryant was officially announced as the MVP Season. "I'm so proud to represent this team to represent this nation." West, responsible for bringing Bryant to the Lakers, took part at the press conference to witness Bryant earning the NBA commissioner David Stern's MVP award. "Kobe deserves it. He had just another great season. Don't surprise me one bit," says Stern. Bryant was the only unanimous selection for the All-NBA team on the 8th of May 2008, for the third straight season and sixth consecutive time in his career and MVP award. He would then lead the NBA All-Defensive First Team alongside Kevin Garnett, taking his 8th award, 52 points, including a record of 24 first-place nodes.

The Lakers finished regular season 2007–08 with a mark of 57–25, ranking first at the Western Conference, and losing against the Nuggets at the first round. In Game 1, Bryant, who said he decoyed most of the game, recorded 18 points of his 32 points in the final eight minutes to comfortably hold Los Angeles away. Denver was the first 50-winner player to be knocked out of the first playoff series since the Grizzlies of Memphis came down in four San Antonio Spurs games in 2004. Bryant recorded 38 points in the first game in the next round against Jazz, while the Lakers defeated Jazz in Game 1. The Lakers also took the next round, then lost Games 3 and 4, despite 33.5 points per game by Bryant. The Lakers secured their semi-finals in the next two days. This created a

Western Conference Final against San Antonio Spurs. The Lakers beat the Spurs in five games against the Boston Celtics, who took part in the NBA Finals. This was the fifth time Bryant has ended the NBA Finals and the first one without O'Neal. In the 2008-2009 season, the Lakers started the campaign by winning their first seven matches in six games. Bryant led the team to equal the franchise record for most of the improvements to start 17–2 and to make a record of 21–3 by mid-December. He has been named a reserve for his eleventh straight All-Star Game, and three times, he has been labeled Western Conference Player of the month in December and January. In a February 2, 2009 match against the Knicks, Bryant posted 61 points during Madison Square Garden. In the 2009 NBA All-Star Game, Bryant was named an All-Star Game co-MVP alongside his former team-mate O'Neal with 27 points, four assists, four blocks, and four steals. In the regular season, the Lakers achieved the West's best record (65–17). Bryant was the second in the MVP vote behind LeBron James and was picked for the 7th time in his career for the All-NBA First Team and All-Defensive First Team.

The Lakers defeated Utah Jazz at the playoffs in five games, and the Houston Rockets at the opening two rounds in seven games. When the Denver Nuggets ended in the six games of the Conference Finals, they got a second straight trip to the NBA Finals. Over five games the Lakers beat the Orlando Magic. Since earning his fourth title, Bryant won his first NBA MVP award, collecting 32.4 points, 7.4 assists, 5.6 rebounds, 1.4 steals and 1.4 blocks. He became the first player since West in the 1969 NBA Finals to average at least 32.4 points and 7.4 assists for a finals series and the first since Jordan to average 30 points, 5 rebounds, and 5 assists for a title-winning team in the finals

During the 2009–10 season, Bryant made six game-winning shots including a buzzer-beating, one-legged 3-pointer against the Miami Heat on December 4, 2009. Bryant considered the shot to be one of his luckiest. A week later, in a contest against the Minnesota Timberwolves, Bryant sustained his right index finger's avulsion fracture. Despite the injury, Bryant chose to continue playing instead of taking time off to recover. Five days after his finger injury, he shot another winner, this time in the overtime game against the Milwaukee Bucks after missing a chance of regulation. Bryant was also the smallest player in his career (31 years, 151 days) to cross 25,000 points over Chamberlain in the season. He continued his successful clutch games by making another three-pointer game against the Sacramento Kings and what a game-winner field goal against the Boston Celtics would be. The next day, he exceeded West to become the leading scorer in the Lakers franchise era. Bryant returned after being injured by an ankle injury for five games and made a further triple clutch to send the Lakers a 1 point lead with four seconds left against Memphis Grizzlies. He made his sixth winning season shot of the Toronto Raptors two weeks later.

Bryant agreed to a three-year contract extension estimated at $87 million on April 2, 2010. Bryant finished the regular season with four of the last five games due to knee and finger injuries. Throughout the season, Bryant suffered multiple injuries and therefore missed nine matches. The Lakers started the playoff as the Number One seed of the Western Conference in six games against the Oklahoma City Thunder. In the second round, the Lakers carried the Utah Jazz to the western conference finals and met the Phoenix Suns. In Game 2, Bryant finished the game with 13 assists, setting up a new high-performance playoff; a Laker playoff performed most since Magic Johnson got 13 in 1996. Over six days, the Lakers won the Western Conference Title and progressed to the NBA Finals for the third straight season. In a match back against the 2008 Boston Celtics champion, Bryant drove Lakers from a 13-point deficiency in Game 7 to win the championship despite shooting 6 for 24. He scored 10 of his game-high 23 points in the 4th trimester and completed with 15 rebounds. Bryant won his fifth championship and won his second NBA Finals MVP award consecutively. The Lakers played a Game7 against the Boston Celtics in the NBA Finals for the first time. Bryant said that all of his five titles were most rewarding.

Chasing a sixth championship (2010–2013)

Bryant wanted a sixth Jordan championship. The Lakers started their first eight games in the 2010-11 season. Bryant became the youngest player in NBA history to score 26,000 career points in his ninth game of the season, played against the Denver Nuggets. His first triple-double was also recorded since January 21, 2009. On 30 January, he was the youngest player to score 27,000 points against the Celtics. Bryant was one of seven players with at least 25,000 points, 5,000 assists, and 5,000 supporters on February 1, 2011. Bryant recorded 20 of his 23 in the second half in Boston on February 10, as the Lakers rallied from an early 15-point loss for 92-86 wins over the Celtics. It was the first win of the Lakers in the season against one of the top four teams in the league, as in previous matches, they were 0–5 and outpaced by a total of 11 points. Bryant, named the lead voting leader in his 13th consecutive All-Star game, had 37 points, 14 assists, and three steals in the 2011 All-Star Game. He also earned his 4th All-Star MVP, matching Famer Hall to Bob Pettit in his most All-Star MVP honors. Bryant rose to the all-time career scoreboard of the NBA from 12th to 6th during the year and jumped by John Havlicek, Dominique Wilkins, Oscar Robertson, Hakeem Olajuwon, Elvin Hayes, and Moses Malone. Bryant completed less than 20 shots a season, his last since the 2003–04 season.

On 13 April 2011, the NBA suspended Bryant $100,000 for pointing a gay slur at the upset official Bennie Adams last day. The NBA's decision to excellent Bryant was praised by the Gay and Lesbian Alliance Against Defamation, and the human rights campaign claimed that Bryant's language was "disgusting." Bryant said that he was open to talking with gay rights groups about the issue and decided to appeal. He subsequently apologized for using the term. Bryant and other Lakers appeared in an announcement from Lakers that denounced his behavior. The franchise hunt for another three-piece ended when the Dallas Mavericks rolled in in the second round of the playoffs, where Bryant underwent groundbreaking platelet-rich plasma treatment in Germany named Orthokine to relieve his left knee and ankle injury and Mike Brown replaced retired Jackson as an off-season assistant for the Lakers. Bryant started playing with an injured wrist in the season. Bryant posted 48 points against the Suns on January 10, 2012. "Too terrible for the seventh best player in the league," Bryant said, pointing to the NBA's top players ' ESPNpre-saison list.

In his next three games, he scored 40, 42 and 42. He recorded 40 or more points in four straight games for the sixth time in his career; this achievement was surpassed only by Chamberlain (19 times). Bryant recorded 27 points for Jordan as the career-scoring leader in the All-Star Game at the 2012 NBA All-Star Game. In the third quarter of the All-Star Game after a hard foul by Dwyane Wade, he has suffered a broken nose and a concussion. Bryant missed seven games in April with a bruised left glow. He played before the end of the regular season for three appearances. He chose not to take on a third NBA scoring title in the final game of the regular season, with 38 points needed to surpass Kevin Durant. The Lakers were knocked out in the second-round playoffs by Durant's Oklahoma City Thunder, losing in five games.

The Lakers recruited Dwight Howard Center and Steve Nash Point Guard in 2012-2013. Bryant recorded 40 points with two steals on 2 November 2012, passing the leader in deals in Lakers, Magic Johnson (1,724). The Lakers, however, lost the Clippers ' game and began the 0-3 season for the first time in 34 and only the fourth time in franchise history. Coach Brown was dismissed after the beginning of season 1–4. He was replaced by Mike D'Antoni, who, when Bryant's dad played in Italy, knew Bryant as a child, and D'Antoni was a star there. Bryant had become the youngest

(34 years and 104 days) player in league history to reach 30 000 points on December 5 versus New Orleans, joining Hall of fame Chamberlain, Jordan, Kareem Abdul-Jabbar, and Karl Malone as one of five players to achieve the landmark. On December 18, in a win of 101 to 100 over Charlotte Bobcats, Bryant recorded a further 30 points in his 7th consecutive game, the longest streak of an NBA player since age 34. On December 28, his streak was snapped by a 104–87 win over the Portland Trail Blazers, and he scored 27 points for the entire fourth quarter. D'Antoni began Bryant to guard the opponent's best perimeter player in a move to improve the team's defense, while Kyrie Irving, the leading defender of the Cavaliers, was held in 15 points. Bryant acknowledged that he was a more vigorous defender than when he played the ball against weaker players when he did a tough defensive assignment. His agitation annoyed rivals and freed Nash from challenging contests, and Bryant guided the Liga to win many of the first 42 points. With a cynical beginning of 17–25, D'Antoni made Bryant become the primary offensive facilitator, and Nash had been pushed off the court to become a spot-up sniper. In the next three tournaments, Bryant had at least 10 participants throughout three victories with a minimum of 39 players, most of them in his lifetime. In every season, he missed a triple-double with nine rebounds twice and eight times. He earned at least 40 points in two critical victories in March with ten assists

in back-to-back games and became the first Laker to accomplish the feat since West in 1970.

With the Lakers fighting in the West Conference for the eighth and final playoff berth and the team injuries, Bryant started playing almost every 48 minutes. The first NBA player in history to have 47 points, eight assists, five aides, four blocks and three steals in an NBA game was Bryant on 10 April 2013. On the 12th of April, Bryant sustained a torn Achilles tendon at the close of his season against the Golden State Warriors. His injury came as he completed seven straight quarters and seven consecutive games for at least 40 minutes. The 34-year-old Bryant was six years old, averaging his most minutes (38.6), and only Portland's rookie Damian Lillard was longer. The General Manager of Lakers, Mitch Kupchak, had spoken to Bryant about his time ten days earlier, but Bryant focused on the minutes needed to continue with the Lakers ' quest for the postseason. On April 13, Bryant had a procedure to patch the tear, and it was reported that six or nine months would be lost. His usual number finished the season, recording a total of 27.3 points, 46.3% shots, 5.6 rebounds, and six assists. The New York Times, though, named his performance in Playoffs "maybe the most outstanding work of his life." Eight times over the season, he hit 40, and eleven times he had a record of 10 or more assists in his role as a dealer nicknamed "Magic Mamba," despite Magic Johnson's passing skills. Bryant's contribution was the second-highest of his career, and his number of field goals was the best since 2008-09. The Lakers ended 45-37 in the season, putting them 7th in the South. In the first round of playoffs, Bryant appeared without Bryant, and in four games, the Lakers were defeated by the San Antonio Spurs in the torn Achilles tendon with April 2013, Bryant worked hard to go back to court until his ACL was only damaged in six games in the 2013-2014 season. In December 2014, the former Al-Star exceeded Michael Jordan for a third time on the NBA scoring list, but his season ends with injury in January 2015 for the third straight year.

Injury-plagued years (2013–2015)

In November 2013, after the 2013–2014 season, Bryant resumed practice. On November 25, he reached a two-year contract extension with the Lakers at an estimated value of $48.5 million. He remains the league's highest-paid player, while he rejected a reduced deal; he had been eligible to receive a contract beginning at $32 million per year. Bryant's salary became a polarizing topic, with critics suggesting that players would take less money to give their team more financial flexibility, while proponents argued that the NBA's biggest stars were compensated less than their real value. After the first 19 games of the season, Bryant resumed playing on December 8. On December 17, Bryant tied his season high of 21 points in a 96–92 victory over Memphis, but he sustained a lateral tibial plateau fracture of his left knee that was supposed to disable him for six weeks. He had started six games after recovering from his Achilles injury, which included action at point guard following injuries to Nash, Steve Blake, and Jordan Farmar. Bryant had a total of 13.8, 6.3 and 4.3 rebounds. Although set aside, fans voted him to start his 16th All-Star game. Bryant did not feel he was worthy of the nomination, and some compared it to a lifetime achievement award for his past performance. He missed the game, however, still being hampered by his knee. On March 12, 2014, the Lakers ruled Bryant out for the remainder of the season, noting his need for more treatment and the limited time left in the season. At the moment, the squad was 22–42 and tied for the worst record in the Western Conference. The Lakers finished 27-55 and for the first time since 2005 they missed playoffs.

Bryant returned for the 2014–15 season, his 19th season with the Lakers, who had substituted D'Antoni with Bryant's old Lakers colleague, Byron Scott. On November 30th, Bryant posted his 20th triple-double career on a 129-122 overtime victory against the

Toronto Raptors with 31 points, 12 assists and 11 rebounds. At 36 years of age, he was the first NBA player to reach 30 points, ten rebounds and ten gambling assists. On December 14, Bryant became the third-highest player of the NBA all-time and won Jordan (32,292) versus Minnesota in a 100-94 victory. He appeared in the first 27 season games, scoring 26.4 points and 35.4 minutes of team-highs per game, leading the league with 22.4 shots per game. But Scott avoided him for three straight games, following one of his worst games of the season, as Bryant made nine turns and recorded 25 points on just 8-for-30 attempts in Sacramento's 108-101 defeat. He hurt in his elbows, feet, the spine, and Achilles' tendons, and Scott intended to reduce his workload. Bryant had gone over 40 minutes three times, and the coach blamed him for having overloaded him after he had begun the season so well. For the season, Bryant only shot 37 percent, and the team only recorded 8–19. In his second game, he had 23 points, 11 assists, and 11 rebounds and was only the third player in the League's history who recorded several triple-doubles in a season at 36 or older. On 21 January 2015, Bryant was hit with a break in the rotator's right arm when working baseline against the Pelicans of New Orleans. Although he was right, he returned and directed the attack with his left hand nearly entirely while firing, dribbling, and throwing. Bryant had been rested in 8 out of 16 games before the injury. He received seasonal surgery for the damage and finished the season with an average of 22.3 points but fired a mediocre 37.3 percent career well under his 45.4 percent mark to get the season started. It was scheduled to sideline for nine months, with a return to early 2015-16. The Lakers ended the season with 21–61 marks, which surpassed the franchise record for most of the defeats in the year before.

The final season (2015–2016)

After recovering from his preseason 2015-16, Bryant suffered a veal injury and missed the exhibition's last two weeks. Nevertheless, he appeared in the opening season to start his 20th season with the Lakers and, for most seasons, surpassed John Stockton's league record of 19 with the same franchise. The Lakers dropped to 2–12 on November 24, 2015, following 111–77 to the Warriors. Bryant just recorded four points in 25 minutes on a 1-for-14 aim, tying his career's most mediocre shoot performance in which he took at least five attempts. Bryant played his final game against his home town team, The Philadelphia 76ers, on December 1, 2015 and the Lakers lost their 103-91 game On November 29, 2015, the Players ' Tribune announced Bryant would retire by the end of the season. Bryant wrote in his poem named "Dear Basketball" that he fell in love with the game at the age of six; "A Love So intensely, I gave you all of my mind/body / To my core." The 2015-2016 season "is all I left to give./My heart can get the beating of my mind / but my body knows it's time to say goodbyes. His free throw attempts dropped on his career level, and his game was overdependent on pump fakes and long-range shots, producing a League-worst of 19.5 percent in the three-point area when playing seven times, almost twice his total. He recognized his deteriorating abilities in his press conference after the declaration. He said Bryant told the opposing teams on the road not to conduct any on-court honors in his name or make any presents to him official. "While I play like garbage, I have worked so hard not to play like crap, and I do whatever I can. Until announcing his retirement, he had been adamant in not wanting to hear boos in favor of cheers on a romantic farewell tour. He was still celebrated worldwide, including in historical places such as the Wells Fargo Center in Philadelphia, the Vivint Smart Home Arena in Salt Lake, TD Garden in Boston, and the Sleep Train Arena Sacramento, with his visual tributaries and his crowd ovations. Bryant was previously respected but not loved, and he was amazed at the cheer he received.

On February 3, Bryant won seven three-pointers and scored an up-and-coming38-point season for the Minnesota Timberwolves 119-115 points out of the team's 18 in the last 5:02 of the game. The victory ended with a 10-game loss string, and the Lakers avoided the longest loss string in franchise history. Bryant was only the fourth NBA player over 37 to record at least 35 points, five rebounds, and five-game helps. With 1,9 million votes, Bryant was the top total candidate for the 2016 All-Star Game ahead of Stephen Curry's 1,6 million ballots. Since switching to small that season, Bryant was picked for the first time as a frontcourt starter. Bryant had 10 points, six rebounds, and seven assists in his first All-Star since 2013. West teammates offered to feed him the ball to try another All-Star MVP, but he refused.

In his last NBA match on April 13, Bryant recorded 60 points against Utah, outscoring the whole jazz side 23–21 in the fourth quarter, with a win of 101–96 from Lakers. He was the first player to score 60 points or more in a game at 37 and 234. The Lakers ended the season with 17–65, their lowest mark in franchise history.

National team career

Bryant refused to play at the 2000 Olympics because he plans to get married during the off-season. He has decided not to participate in the FIBA World Championship in 2002. Bryant was initially selected for the 2003 FIBA Americas Championship but withdrew after arthroscopic knee and shoulder surgery. In the following summer, thanks to his sexual assault lawsuit, he had to remove from the Olympic team. Together with LeBron James, he was one of two first stars to be identified officially by Jerry Colangelo in the 2006–2008 US provisional roster. However, after knee surgery, he was sidelined again, not participating in the 2006 FIBA World Championship.

Bryant's national team tenure in the United States finally began in 2007. He was a member of the 2007 USA Men's Senior National Team and the USA FIBA America Championship Team, a 10-0 winner and a United States men qualifier for the 2008 Olympics. He started in all 10 FIBA Americas games of the USA. Bryant scored 15.3 points in the tournament, 2.9 assists, 2.0 blocks, and 1.6 robs a game.

On June 23, 2008, he had been selected to the US Men's Senior National Team for the 2008 Summer Olympics. Bryant tallied 20 points, including 13 in the fourth quarter, along with six assists, as Team USA beat Spain 118–107 in the gold medal game on August 24, 2008, for its first gold medal in a worldwide tournament since the 2000 Olympics. He recorded 15.0 points, 2.8 blocks, and 2.1 assists while shooting.462 from the field in eight Olympic contests.

Since earning another gold medal, Bryant decided to retire from the program. He ended his national team tenure by a record of 26-0 in 3 competitions, each time he took out a gold medal.

Basketball legacy

Adam Silver, NBA commissioner and the New York Times, called Bryant "one of the best players in our game's history," and Reuters called him "one of the sport's most decorated careers." Reuters called him "surely the best player of his generation," while Sporting News and TNT named him their NBA player for the 2000s. ESPN ranked him the second-biggest shooting guard after Jordan in 2008 and again in 2016. Their age's Jordanian variant was dubbed Bryant by celebrities like Kevin Durant, Dirk Nowitzki, Dwyane Wade, and Derrick Rose. The press company described Bryant as "perhaps the biggest Laker in the history of the organization." He was the forever leading scorer in Lakers, and his five championships are the most associated in franchise history. On 18 December 2017, the Lakers removed all his numbers throughout his service, 8 and 24.

He was considered one of the NBA's most successful players with a career average of 25.0 points, 5.2 rebounds, 4.7 assists, and 1.4 steals per game. He was the first player in the NBA history to have at least 30 thousand career points and at least 6000 career support and was one of just four players with 25 thousand points, 6 thousand rebounds, and 6 thousand assists. In the 2005–06 and 2006–07 seasons, Bryant dominated the League. His 81-point Toronto performance in 2006 was the second-highest in NBA history behind Chamberlain's 100. He scored 24 times at least 50 points, the seventh in Jordan's league history (31), and Chamberlain (118); Bryant has scored at least 60 times. He was only the third player in the NBA's history to achieve an average of 40 points over a calendar month four times. In 2008, Bryant was elected to the MVP league and led his team to the 2008 NBA Final as the Western Conference's first seed. He was given a Gold Medal in the 2008 Summer Olympics as a part of the U.S. men's basketball team, referred to as "The Redeem Squad." At the 2012 Summer Olympics, he earned another gold medal. Throughout 2009 and 2010, he guided the Lakers to two more titles, each winning the final MVP award.

Bryant was an 18-time All-Star, second behind just the 19th Kareem Abdul-Jabbar. He was picked as an unprecedented 18 times straight, each time as a starter. He was the top candidate four times (2003, 2011, 2013, 2016). The All-Star MVP was named Bryant four times, a mark which he shares with Bob Pettit. He has been selected for the All-NBA team 15 times, often associated with Abdul-Jabbar and Tim Duncan, and his 11 first-team awards are related to Karl

Malone in second place. He's also a 12-time All-Defensive Team team that lacks Duncan's 15 and has been named the First All-Defensive Team nine times and has been mainly linked to Jordan, Garnett, and Gary Payton. He was the first player to play in the NBA for 20 seasons. He was the youngest winner of the NBA Slam Dunk Contest in 1997. Bryant earned 40-plus in 121 games and posted a triple-double 21 times in his career.

After his death, Commissioner Adam Silver announced on 15 February 2020 that he would re-title the NBA All-Star Game MVP Award to the Kobe Bryant Most Valuable NBA All-Star Game in honor of Bryant.

List of career achievements by Kobe Bryant

Kobe Bryant was a shooting guard at the National Basketball Association (NBA)'s Los Angeles Lakers during his 20-year tenure. A month later, Bryant was picked 13th overall by the Charlotte Hornets in the NBA 1996 draft to the Los Angeles Lakers for Vlade Divac. He and then Shaquille O'Neal led the Lakers to three consecutive NBA championships between 2000 and 2002. After the 2003-04 season in which O'Neal was traded to the Miami Heat, Bryant became the Lakers leader. He dominated the League in the 2005-2006 and 2006-2007 seasons. In 2006, Bryant posted 81 points on the Toronto Raptors, the second-highest in

NBA history, only the 100-point performance of Wilt Chamberlain and the most production for a forward. Bryant was given the Most Valuable Player Award in the 2007–08 season for the regular season and was the first pick for his team in the Western Conference at the 2008 NBA Finals. Bryant was the twice Olympic Gold Medalist, a member of the U.S. men's basketball team, starting in the 2008 Summer Olympics ("The Redeem Team") and following the 2012 Summer Olympics Team. Throughout 2009 and 2010, he guided the Lakers to two more victories, earning the Finals MVP Trophy.

Bryant is currently ranked fourth in the all-time post-season scoring table and all-time regular-season score charts. He was picked by 15 teams (eleven times in the Team First All-NBA) and 12 teams for Offense (nine times for the Team First All-Defensive). He was chosen to play in the NBA All-Star Game 18 times and was the winner of the All-Star MVP Award in 2002, 2007, 2009, and 2011. In 2020, the award would be named for him. Throughout 1997, he won the NBA Slam Dunk Contest and the Rookie Game MVP. It's recorded 180-point, 660-point (including its final), 26 50-point, and 134 40-point games throughout his career. Kobe was also on a three-way tie with Stephen Curry and Donyell Marshall for most three-pointers, 12 of whom in a season, before Curry registered 13 on November 8, 2016. At the age of 37, he became the first player to score 60 in the same game on April 13, 2016, and reached the highest peak in the regular season 2015-16.

NBA awards and accomplishments

• 5-time NBA champion: 2000, 2001, 2002, 2009, 2010

• 7 NBA Finals appearances: 2000, 2001, 2002, 2004, 2008, 2009, 2010

• 2-time NBA Finals MVP: 2009, 2010

• NBA Most Valuable Player: 2008

• 2-time scoring champion: 2006, 2007

• 18-time NBA All-Star: 1998, 2000, 2001, 2002, 2003, 2004, 2005, 2006, 2007, 2008, 2009, 2010, 2011, 2012, 2013, 2014, 2015, 2016

• 18 consecutive selections, 13 consecutive appearances (No All-Star game in 1999 due to a league-wide lockout)

• Missed 2010, 2014 and 2015 games due to injury

• 4-time NBA All-Star Game MVP: 2002, 2007, 2009, 2011 (shared the 2009 award with Shaquille O'Neal)

15-time All-NBA Team selection:

• First team: 2002, 2003, 2004, 2006, 2007, 2008, 2009, 2010, 2011, 2012, 2013

• Second team: 2000, 2001

• Third team: 1999, 2005

• 12-time All-Defensive Team selection:

• First team: 2000, 2003, 2004, 2006, 2007, 2008, 2009, 2010, 2011

• Second team: 2001, 2002, 2012

• NBA All-Rookie Team selection:

• Second team: 1997

• NBA Slam Dunk Contest champion: 1997

• 34-time Player of the Month: December 2000, November 2001, January 2003, March 2004, January 2006, April 2006, December 2006, March 2007, April 2007, February 2008, April 2008, December 2008, January 2009, December 2009, March 2011, December/January 2012, February 2013

• Player of the Month was awarded separately to Eastern and Western Conference starting from the 2001–02 season.

NBA regular season leader:

• games played: 1998–99 (50), 2007–08 (82), 2008–09 (82)

• usage percentage: 2005–06 (38.7), 2010–11 (35.1), 2011–12 (35.7)

• points: 2002–03 (2,461), 2005–06 (2,832, 7th in NBA history),[30] 2006–07 (2,430), 2007–08 (2,323)

• points per game: 2005–06 (35.4, 8th in NBA history),[31] 2006–07 (31.6)

• field goals attempted: 2005–06 (2,173), 2006–07 (1,757), 2007–08 (1,690), 2010–11 (1,639), 2011–12 (1336)

• field goals made: 2002–03 (868), 2005–06 (978), 2006–07 (813)

• free throws attempted: 2006–07 (768)

• free throws made: 2005–06 (696), 2006–07 (667)

• 2nd most points in a game: 81 (on January 22, 2006 vs. the Toronto Raptors)

• 2x Best NBA Player ESPY Award winner: 2008, 2010

NBA playoffs leader:

• win shares: 2001 (3.8)

• points: 2004 (539), 2008 (633), 2009 (695), 2010 (671)

• points per game: 2003 (32.1), 2007 (32.8), 2008 (30.1)

• minutes played: 2002 (833), 2004 (973)

• field goals made: 2004 (190), 2008 (222), 2009 (242), 2010 (234)

• field goals attempted: 2002 (431), 2004 (460), 2008 (463), 2009 (530), 2010 (511)

• free throws made: 2004 (135), 2008 (157), 2009 (174), 2010 (154)

• free throws attempted: 2008 (194), 2010 (183)

• steals: 2000 (32), 2009 (38)

• turnovers: 2010 (79)

• personal fouls: 2000 (89)

NBA records

Bryant holds or shares numerous NBA records:

• Most Seasons played for a single NBA Franchise: 20 (tied with Dirk Nowitzki)

• Most All-Star Game MVP awards won, career: 4 (tied with Bob Pettit)

• Most offensive rebounds in an All-Star Game: 10

• Most All-NBA Total Selections won, career: 15 (tied with Kareem Abdul-Jabbar and Tim Duncan)

• Most All-NBA First Team honors won, career: 11 (tied with Karl Malone and LeBron James)

• Most All-Defensive First Team honors won, career: 9 (tied with Michael Jordan, Gary Payton, and Kevin Garnett)

• Most free throws made, four-game playoff series: 51 (second round vs. Sacramento Kings, 2001)

• Most points scored in one arena, career: 16,161 (as of April 14, 2016, at Staples Center, Los Angeles)

• Most games played at one arena, career: 599 (as of April 14, 2016, at Staples Center, Los Angeles

• Highest Score against rest of teams in the league above 40 (share with Bob Pettit)

• Surpassed Hakeem Olajuwon, the previous holder of the record

• Youngest player to score 32,000 points: (36 years, 87 days)

• Surpassed Karl Malone, the previous holder of the record

• Youngest player to score 33,000 points: (37 years, 138 days)

• Surpassed Kareem Abdul-Jabbar, the previous holder of the record

• Youngest player to be named to the NBA All-Rookie Team: (1996–97)

• Youngest player to be named to the NBA All-Defensive Team: (1999–00)

• Youngest player to start a game: (18 years, 158 days)

• Youngest player to win the NBA Slam Dunk Championship: (18 years, 169 days)

• Youngest player to start an All-Star game: (19 years, 169 days)

• Only player in NBA history to score at least 600 points in the postseason for three consecutive years.

• 633 (2008), 695 (2009), 671 (2010)

• Oldest player to score 60+ points, one game: (37 years, 234 days)

• Most total playoff CP with 3800

• Highest CPPG with 20 cppg

Bryant Retirement

Bryant was back in time for the start of the NBA season 2015-2016, but he fought with his young teammates from Lakers. He announced in November 2015 that he would retire at the end of the season. "It's all that I have left to give this season," he posted on the website The Players ' Tribune. "My heart may get the blowing. My mind will live with the blowing, so my body knows that it is time to say goodbye," said NBA Commissioner Adam Silver. "Kob Bryant is one of the best players in the history of the game with 17 NBA All-Star picks and a Finals MVP, five NBA Lakers titles, two Olympic gold medals, and an unwavering professional ethic," said Silver in a statement. "Either playing in final or running in an empty gym, Kobe has a pure love for the game," said Bryant on April 12, 2016. He recorded sixty points and guided the Lakers to victory over Utah Jazz in a sold-out stadium at the Staples Center and supporters everywhere in the last game of his career. It was the sixth game of Bryant's 60-point career.

Bryant spoke to the audience after the contest. "I can't believe how easily 20 years have passed," he added. "This's completely crazy... and to sit in the center court with you, my friends behind me, appreciating the journey we have been moving on — we have been through our ups and downs. I believe that the best thing we all had together throughout." Bryant, like O'Neal, Phil Jackson, Pau Gasol, Derek Fisher, Lamar O, has also given a salute to an all-star line-up with Laker legends. "We have been here for 20 years to honor success," said Johnson. "Excellence for twenty years. Kobe Bryant has never been able to trick the game; he has never tricked us as supporters. He played with pain; he played an accident.

PERSONAL LIFE

Bryant encountered 17-year-old Vanessa Laine in November 1999, as an extra dancer in the "G'd Up" music video of Tha Eastsidaz. Bryant focused on his first musical album in the house. Six months later, all started dating in May 2000, when Laine was still a student at Huntington Beach Marina High School in California. To stop media scrutiny, she worked privately at high school. There was no prenuptial agreement, according to Vanessa's sister Laila Laine. Bryant said, "too much for her for one," Vanessa said.

They met at St. Edward Catholic Church in Dana Point, California, on April 18, 2001. Bryant's father, his two brothers, a former friend, and negotiator Arn Tellem and his Laker teammates did not participate in the ceremony. For many reasons, Bryant's parents rejected marriage. Bryant's parents reportedly had difficulty marrying him too young, especially a woman who wasn't an African American. This disagreement culminated in a two-year estrangement era, which ended when the first daughter of the couple was born.

Wife and Kids

Bryant married 19-year-old Vanessa Laine in April 2001. The couple became parents to four daughters:

Natalia Diamante (b. 2003), Gianna Maria-Onore (b. 2006, d. 2020), Bianka (b. 2016) and Capri (b. 2019).

The first child of Bryants was named in January 2003. The birth leads to Bryant's reunion with his father. Vanessa suffered a miscarriage in the spring of 2005 as a consequence of an ectopic pregnancy. Gianna was born in May 2006, their second daughter. Vanessa Bryant filed a divorce on 16 December 2011, citing irreconcilable differences, and the couple applied for their daughters ' joint custody. On 11 January 2013, Bryant and his wife also revealed that they had ended their divorce via social media. Vanessa gave birth to her third daughter in early December 2016, and in January 2019, the Bryants revealed they were expecting a fourth. In June 2019, their daughter was born.

Bryant was a Protestant studying. He said his religion and a priest guided him to navigate difficult times, like the period after being accused of rape. A Catholic cantor said she was inspired by the faith and respect of Bryant. Bryant and his family regularly attended the Newport Beach Catholic Church of Our Lady Queen of Angels. Only hours before he died of a helicopter crash, Bryant and Gianna entered the Eucharist together.

Bryant was multilingual. He was multilingual. He fluently talked English, Italian, and Spanish. Bryant called himself "Black Mamba" and alluded to his desire for the basketball skills to imitate the potential of his eponymous snake to "hit at maximum speed and in quick succession with 99 percent precision." In the 2012–2013 season, he began calling himself "vino" to describe how his performance was aged like a fine wine.

Bryant purchased a $4 million Mediterranean property on the Newport Bay, Newport Beach cul-de-sac, in January 2002. In May 2015, he sold the house.

Throughout 2013, Bryant had a legal dispute with an auction house about his early years' memorabilia that his mother auctioned. Mother Bryant got $450,000 for the items from the auction house and argued Bryant had entitled her to the details he had lived in her residence. Yet Bryant's lawyers demanded that the auction house return the pieces. A settlement was reached before the scheduled jury, requiring the auction house to sell fewer than 10% of the products. Bryant's parents excused him in a written statement for the dispute and thanked the financial support he had received for them over the years.

Bryant was a lifelong supporter of Philadelphia Eagles, his local NFL team. He was also a supporter of

Barcelona, AC Milan, and Manchester City football teams.

According to Forbes, the total worth of Bryant was valued at 350 million dollars in 2016 and placed him #10 on the world's top-paid athlete chart.

Bryant Sexual Assault Charge

In July 2003, Bryant was accusing a 19-year-old hotel contractor in Colorado with a sexual assault. He was guilty of adultery, Bryant said, but he was innocent of the charge of rape. The complaint against Bryant was dropped in 2004, and the Hotel Worker's civil lawsuit against him resolved out of court.

Eagle County Sheriff prosecutors first approached Bryant with a sexual assault charge on 2 July 2003. In the July 2003 interview with the authorities, Bryant also told the investigators that he had no contact with his victim, a 19-year older woman who worked in Bryant's hotel. When the officers told Bryant she had an interview of physical evidence including sperm, Bryant acknowledged that she had intercourse with her but claimed the sex was consensual. When asked about the blowbags in the accuser's neck, Bryant admitted to "strangling" her at her meeting, saying that he kept her "around her neck" from the "back," that sex was his "thing" and that during her recurred sexual encounters he had a pattern of strangling another sex partner, (not his wife). When asked how hard he held onto his neck, Bryant said, "My hands are strong. I don't know." Bryant declared he accepted sex because of the body language of the accuser.

Law enforcement officers collected Bryant's evidence and agreed to submit a rape test kit and a voluntary polygraph test. Sheriff Joe Hoy issued a warrant for Bryant on 4 July. Bryant flew back to Eagle, Colorado, from Los Angeles to surrender to the police. He was immediately released on a $25,000 bond, and two days later, news of the arrest was made public. The Eagle District Attorney's office lodged a formal charge of sexual assault against Bryant on 18 July. Bryant faced probation for life in prison if convicted. On July 18, Bryant held a news conference after formally charging and denying he had raped the woman. He acknowledged that he had an illicit sexual encounter with her.

Pre-trial trials were conducted in December 2003 to make appeals on facts admissible. During those trials, the prosecutors suspected Bryant's defense team of undermining his defendant's reputation. It has been shown that the day after the alleged incident, she wore underwear, including the sperm of another individual and pubic hair in her rape test. Detective Doug Winters has confirmed that her yellow panties, along with the Caucasian pubic hair, included another man's sperm. Bryant's response argued that the investigation's findings showed "strong evidence of innocence" since the victim had another sexual encounter after the accident. She advised the researchers that she mistakenly took dirty underwear from her laundry basket when she left the house for study. She said that she hadn't showered since the morning of the incident, the day she was examined. The study showed signs of genital abuse alleged by the Bryant defense team to have sex with multiple partners in two days.

The police evidence contained Bryant's T-shirt on the night of the incident, which had three small blood stains on it. The smudge was identified as DNA testing of the accuser's blood and therefore was not menstrual blood because the accuser claimed that she had her blood two weeks earlier. It was discovered that Bryant bent the woman over a chair to have sex with her, potentially triggering the damage. That's the sex act, as the accuser claims that she told Bryant to stop, but he did not, and Bryant claims that he quit after he asked whether he could ejaculate on her face.

Trina McKay, auditor of the resort at night, said she saw the accuser going home, and "she didn't look or sound like there was any problem." Bobby Pietrack, a secondary school friend and bellman at the pool, said that she seemed angry and "told me that Kobe Bryant had subjected her to sex."

A few weeks before the jury was set to occur, the defendant wrote a letter to state prosecutor Gerry

Sandberg sharing several information about her first Colorado police interview. She said, "I said to Detective Winters that while I was leaving, I had car problems that morning, that was not true; when I called late to work that day it was why I offered my manager the chance to be late, I overslept I told Detective Winters that Mr. Bryant had made me sit in the room to wash my face. Twice the woman was trying to destroy herself in school by overdosing the sleeping pills, Lindsey McKinney, who stayed with the defendant. Before the accident, the victim, a singer in charge, attempted American Idol on TV for Rebecca Lynn Howard's single "Forgive," but couldn't push on. In addition to Bryant's defense lawyer's moral character and reputation, her death threats and hatred mail were received, and her identity was leaked several times.

On 1 September 2004, Eagle District Judge Terry Ruckriegle rejected Bryant's charges, having spent more than $200,000 preparing for trial because their prosecutor informed them of their unwillingness to testify.

The same day as the court case was dismissed, Bryant issued the following statement to his lawyer: First of all, I would like to apologize to the young lady directly involved. I want to apologize to her for this evening's actions and the repercussions of the past year. Although it was incredibly hard for me to endure this year personally, I can only imagine the pain it suffered. I would also like to apologize to her aunt and colleagues, my mates, friends, and supporters, as well as the residents of Eagle, Colorado.

I also want to make it clear that I am not concerned about this young woman's motivations. This woman was paying no rent. She has agreed that in the civil case, this declaration will not be used against me. Although I genuinely think that the discussion between us was consensus-based, I now understand that she did not treat this event like I did. After months of reviewing her findings, listening to her lawyer, and even her testimony, I now understand how she feels she has not consented to this meeting.

Today I am fully aware that while one aspect of this case ends today, another one continues. I agree the civil case against me is going to continue. In August 2004, the accuser filed a civil proceeding against Bryant over the incident and between the parties directly concerned by the event, which no longer constitutes a financial or emotional drain to the citizens of the state of Colorado. All sides settled the case in March 2005. The terms of the deal were not publicly disclosed. The Los Angeles Times reported that the settlement was estimated at more than 2.5 million dollars by law experts.

Eight months after the incident, Cordillera's Lodge & Spa has rebuilt and sold some furniture as part of it. There was speculation that some items from room 35 included in this sale were supposed to have been stayed by Kobe Bryant. The lodge rejected this and said he had disposed of the furniture separately from the room. The hotel was closed in 2019 and is now a medical treatment center.

Despite these claims, Bryant negotiated a seven-year contract worth $136 million for seven years, and he recovered some of his trademarks from Adidas, Spalding, and Coca-Cola despite not having extended his terms with products including Nutella and McDonald's.

ENDORSEMENTS

Before the 1996-97 season started, Bryant agreed with Nike a six-year deal worth around $48 million. Gear KB 8 was his first trademark pair. Bryant's other earlier approvals included the Coca-Cola Company deals to support their Sprite soft drink, ads for McDonald's advertisements, and Spalding's latest NBA Infusion Ball, Upper Deck, Italian chocolate company Ferrero SpA's Nutella brand, Russell Company, and Nintendo's own video game series. Several businesses, such as McDonald's and Ferrero SpA, terminated their relationships after rape claims against him were made public. One significant exception was Adidas, Inc., which had negotiated a $40-45 million deal for five years just before the event. They declined to use a new shoe of his name or sell it for the year but finally started selling Bryant only two years when his image came back. Since then, he has managed to sign up for The Coca-Cola Company's Energy Brands division, to support their Vitamin Water drinks line. Bryant was also the NBA ' 07 cover athlete with the Life Vol. 2 and published in 2008 in the video game Guitar Hero World Tour (together with Tony Hawk, Michael Phelps, and Alex Rodriguez) and 2010.

Bryant seems to jump over a fast-moving Aston Martin in a 2008 video promoting Nike's Hyperdunk shoes. The prank was deemed suspect, and the Los Angeles Times said a real hoax was possibly an infringement of the Bryant's Lakers deal. Following Nike's Hyperdunk Boots, Jackson came out with Nike's fourth signature line, The Zoom Kobe IV. In 2010 Nike launched another Shoe, the Nike Zoom Kobe V. In 2009, the Sports / Luxury watch brand, which ranged from $25,000 to $285.000, was negotiated a distribution contract with Nubeo for the' Black Mamba ' series. Bryant was featured on the cover of ESPN The Magazine on February 9, 2009. However, it wasn't linked to basketball; instead, Bryant was a great fan of FC Barcelona. In 2007, CNN reported Bryant's funding packages to be $16 million a year. In 2010 Bryant was third in Forbes ' list of the world's highest-paid celebrities with $48 million behind Tiger Woods and Jordan.

Bryant with the United States. President George W. Bush, Jason Kidd, and Deron Williams reached a two-year endorsement deal with Turkey's national airline, Turkish Airlines, on December 13, 2010. Bryant was involved in a promotional film to be broadcast in more than 80 countries and digital, print, and poster publicity.

Bryant appeared as the cover athlete for the following video games:

- Kobe Bryant in NBA Courtside

- NBA Courtside 2: Featuring Kobe Bryant

- NBA Courtside 2002

- NBA 3 On 3 Featuring Kobe Bryant

- NBA '07: Featuring the Life Vol. 2

- NBA '09: The Inside

- NBA 2K10

- NBA 2K17 (Legend Edition; Legend Edition Gold)

In September 2012, Bryant filmed a Turkish Airlines commercial with Lionel Messi, an FC Barcelona player. In the new ad in the carrier, the pair competes to win a young boy's interest. In 2013 Forbes rated Bryant, behind Floyd Mayweather, Cristiano Ronaldo, LeBron James, and Lionel Messi, as the fifth-highest-paying sports star globally.

Bryant also acted as one of the global leaders for China's FIBA World Cup 2019.

MUSIC, FILM, AND OTHER BUSINESS

Bryant was a part of a rap group called CHEIZAW at a secondary school named after the Chi Sah gang in the martial arts movie Kids with the Golden Arm. Sony Entertainment signed the group, but its ultimate objective was to eliminate the group and have Bryant record on its own. Bryant's popularity and NBA fame deserved to be capitalized by the name. He appeared in a 1997 Sway & King Tech concert and released a verse for a version of "Hold Me" by Brian McKnight. Bryant appeared even on O'Neal's Respect teammate Lakers, starting the track "3 X's Dope," although Bryant's name was not credible.

Sony forced Bryant into a radio-friendly style from its underground hip hop origins. In spring 2000, his debut album, Visions, was scheduled for release. The first song, "K.O.B.E'," starred Tyra Banks, the supermodel performing the melody. The song made its debut at the NBA All-Star Weekend in January 2000 and was not widely received. Sony scrapped the album's ambitions, which never came out, and later that year fired Bryant. The president of Sony, who originally signed Bryant, had left, and most of Bryant's other supporters had given up. So Bryant formed an independent record label, Heads High Records, which collapsed into a year. Bryant featured in 1999 on the Maxi single album cover of "Say My Name" by Destiny's Child.

Bryant was mentioned in 2011 on Taiwanese singer Jay Chou's album, "The Heaven and Earth Fight" (Tian Di Yi Dou). Download proceeds for both the collection and ringtones were contributed to disadvantaged basketball and equipment colleges. Bryant also includes the music video of the song. In its 2011 marketing campaign throughout China, Sprite also used the album.

Rapper Lil Wayne called an album "Kobe Bryant" in 2009. Likewise, rapper Sho Baraka has released in 2010, a song called "Kobe Bryant On'em" on his Lions & Liars record.

Television

Bryant made his acting debut in 1996 and appears as part of a Moesha episode (he met Brandy's show star earlier this year during a Nike All-Star basketball game, and then Brandy was Bryant's senior high school date a few months later in May 1996). In 1998, on the Nickelodeon comedy series All That, he appeared on MTV's Ridiculousness in 2019.

Business ventures

Bryant has founded Kobe Inc. to own and grow sports brands. In March 2014, the initial investment amounted to 10 percent of the Bodyarmor SuperDrink Business. The office is located in Newport Beach, California. With The Coca-Cola Company acquiring a minority interest in the enterprise in August 2018, Bryant's stake valuation rose to about 200 million dollars.

Bryant and its business partner Jeff Stibel launched Bryant-Stibel, a venture capital company with a $100 million funding focused on various businesses, including media, data, gaming, and technology.

Film

In 2018 Bryant was the first African American to receive the Academy Prize for Best Animated Short Film and the first former professional player honored for his Dear Basketball film to earn an Academy Award in all categories.

Book

The book The Mamba Mentality: Why I Play by Andrew D. Bernstein, an introduction by Phil Jackson, and a preface by Pau Gasol, was published by MCD / Farrar, Straus, and Giroux on October 23rd, 2018. The book looks back with pictures and memories from his life.

He collaborated with Brazilian author Paulo Coelho on a children's book to empower underprivileged children at his passing. After Bryant died, Coelho deleted his draft, saying in an interview, "it made no sense to publish without him." He did not tell him how many pages were written or if the book had a title.

Philanthropy

Among its philanthropic efforts, the basketball collaborated in the Kobe & Vanessa Bryant Family Foundation with the non-profit Afterschool All-Stars.

Bryant was an honorary Ambassador for All-Stars After School (ASAS), an Independent non-profit organization supplying children in preteen US communities with comprehensive post-school programs. Bryant has also launched the Kobe Bryant China Trust, a foundation funded by the Chinese government and associated with the Soong Ching Ling Foundation. The Kobe Bryant China Fund raises funds for education and health services inside China. On 4 November 2010, Bryant appeared in the "Call of Duty: Black Ops launch event" at Santa Mónica Airport alongside Zach Braff, which was introduced to the "Call of Duty Endowment," a non-profit organization created by the Call of Duty, which supports veterans in returning to civil life after the military service finishes.

Bryant created the Kobe and Vanessa Bryant Family Foundation (KVBFF) together with his partner. Its goals are to "help needy young people develop their physical and social skills through sport and help homeless people." Bryant mentioned the injustice directed at homeless people accused of their situation, stating that homelessness must not be neglected or given low priority. He desired more than a good basketball career from adulthood, Bryant said.

BRYANT'S DEATH

On 26 January 2020, Bryant was on a Sikorsky-76 helicopter crashed in Calabasas ' Los Angeles suburb. Nine people died, including Bryant and Gianna "Gigi," his 13-year old daughter. The helicopter was on its way from Orange County to Thousand Oaks, California, to prepare Bryant for a competition at the Mamba Sports Academy.

On 26 January 2020, 9:06 a.m. PST (17:06 UTC), Bryant departed John Wayne AIRPORT (SNA) in Orange County, California, Sikorsky Helicopter S-76B, listed on N72EX, with eight other men. He had his thirteen-year-old daughter, Gianna, his colleagues, Alyssa Altobelli, the 14-year-old, and the 13-year-old of Payton Chester. They moved to Bryant's Mamba Sports Academy in Newbury Park for a basketball game, where Bryant was hoping to coach Gianna's team. Flight reports show that the day before, the helicopter was flown to Camarillo Airport (CMA), the major general airport in general aviation, some 20 minutes by car from the Mamba Sports Academy. The previous day took just 30 minutes to ride, but it would have received at least two hours to go from Bryant's home in Newport Beach to the academy.

Conditions

The Los Angeles Police Air Support Division grounded the police aircraft for poor weather conditions on 26 January. Air Support Division rules require visibility for at least 2 miles and a cloud limit of 800 feet (240 m). The sight was 5 miles (8.0 km) when N72EX was taken off from SNA, and it was operated on a 14 C.F.R. 135 on-demand passenger flight under visual flight (VFR) regulations by Island Express Helicopters Inc. It is possible to fly through the clouds if a pilot decides to operate according to IFR (Instrument Flight Regulations), but the company's pilots were not permitted to hop on the IFR according to a former Island Express and FAA pilot registers.

Furthermore, a part 135 Operating Certificate issued in 1998 restricted operations to on-demand VFR-only flights. Even if the company had granted IFR operating certificate and rules, this option would have resulted in long delays and delays (using any anticipated time savings) due to severe airspace congestion-controlled from Los Angeles. Bryant's role as a star in that area would not have earned the helicopter preference.

According to an automatic weather station in Van Nuys Airport, the cloud ceiling (below the cloud layer) was 1 100 feet (340 m) above ground level. Closer to the crash site, the top of the cloud extended to 2,400 feet (730 m), meaning that aircraft would be enveloped in clouds between that two altitudes.

Flight

Since a pilot can not fly into or near clouds by visual flight laws, the helicopter has risen to an altitude of 800 feet (240 m) over a mean sea level (amsl) while flying northwest from SNA. The aircraft had been flying to the west of downtown Los Angeles on most of its recent flights to Camarillo, flying over Santa Monica Mountain until it took the Ventura Freeway (US 101). On 26 January, however, this was not an option for VFR flights due to the deep sea shift from the Pacific into the Santa Monica. Instead, the helicopter continued northwest, flew through the Boyle Heights near Dodger Stadium to the Golden State Freeway (I-5) route. As the flight approached Glendale, the pilot requested permission from the Burbank Airport air traffic controllers to follow the Ventura Freeway (USA 101); (17:21 UTC) Until permission is granted at 9:32 a.m. (17:32 UTC) continue to the Burbank Airport controlled airspace.

Permission to continue was issued under special VFR, which allowed the pilot to stay at an altitude of fewer than 2 500 feet (760 m). The aircraft exceeded a height of 430 meters (1,400 feet) above sea level. Following the Ronald Reagan Freeway (SR 118) as it approached the airspace under jurisdiction of the airport of Van Nuys, the Van Nuys controllers shortly after permitted a switch southwest of the Ventura Freeway (US 101) at 9:39 a.m. Pilot Ara Zobayan then reported that he was still in VFR flights at 1,500 feet (460 m) and acknowledged the handoff to air traffic control in Southern California (SCT).

Around 9:42 a.m. (17:42 UTC), the helicopter landed and began following the Ventura Freeway to the west of the San Fernando Valley, approaching more hilly areas on the west side. About 9:44 a.m. The SCT controller told the helicopter that it was too close to the airfield for takeoff, a tracking service that would have given constant verbal alerts on the VFR flight (17:44 UTC), in reaction to a message from the operator. After the ride, the SCT controller stopped and eventually was replaced by another unit. The relief controller told the pilot to identify and question his thoughts because the central SCT controller had been drained. At a press conference, NTSB participant Jennifer Homendy said the pilot had brought the aircraft into a climb to clear a cloud layer of 4,000 feet (1 200 m), the last communication the pilot had carried out.

As the plane began to rise, the aircraft climbed to about 1000 feet (300 m) in 36 seconds. According to transponders, the aircraft then took a descending turn to the left, going south and peaking at 2.300 meters (700 m) above ground level (1.500 feet) before dropping eight seconds later to an altitude of 1.400 meters (430 m); the helicopter then made a further downward turn to the left, continuing southeast. Around 9:45 a.m., the aircraft began a dive. A speed of 160 knots (300 km / h) before it reached the hillside at 9:45:39 a.m. (17:45 UTC), descending at an overall rate of 4,000 ft/min (20 m / s). Approximately 1.085 feet (331 m) height

Impact and emergency response

A 9-1-1 emergency call was reported at 9:47 a.m. The helicopter crashed and caught fire in Calabasas, Calif., near the intersection of Las Virgenes Road and Willow Glen Street. (5:45 PM UTC). The crash took place on a hillside behind the Las Virgin Municipal Water District's offices on the New Millennium Loop Trail. The hill is regulated by both the water district and another governmental agency, known as the Mountains Recreation and Conservation Authority, and is part of a small valley, which is also located at the peak of Malibu Canyon.

At that time, the weather was reported to be foggy in Calabasas. The helicopter descended from two mountain biking parties that called 9-1-1. Witnesses said that the engine of the aircraft "sputtered" before the crash. Others have claimed that the plane falls to the ground at an "equally high pace" clip. It is not known whether a distress call has been made.

The accident ended with a 1/4 acre (1000 m2) forest fire that was hard to extinguish due to magnesium (which interacts with oxygen and water). Firefighters from Los Angeles County Fire Department react, and the fire swept out at 10:30. The crash debris was scattered over a field of 500 to 600 feet (150 to 180 m) in steep terrain. Firefighters rushed to the area and helicopter-recalled doctors to the site but could not locate any survivors; all nine helicopter passengers were killed in the crash. Following tests by the Department of Clinical Examining and Coroner in Los Angeles County, nine people were killed by blunt trauma.

Aircraft

The Sikorsky S-76B was owned by the State of Illinois until 2015 and used to carry governors and other authorities. The helicopter was licensed with the Island Express Holding Company in Fillmore, California, according to the FAA and California Secretary of State documents. Twelve (as N761LL) passenger seating on the helicopter is turned into eight after selling to Island Express. It was not usually known if Bryant chartered or leased the full aircraft time following the crash.

The aircraft did not have a flight data recorder (FDR) or a CVR; the U.S. is not obligated to carry helicopters. Although the S-76B originally had a CVR installed, the records show that Island Express was removed from its CVR shortly after purchasing a helicopter from the State of Illinois in March 2016. The helicopter was also not equipped with a Terrain conscience and warning system (TAWS).

Reporting and investigation

TMZ was the first news source to report Bryant's death fewer than two hours after the accident at 11.24 a.m. The local authorities also blamed TMZ for publishing the story before the coroner service could ascertain the identity of the passengers of the helicopter and notify their relatives. Alex Villanueva, Los Angeles County Sheriff, states,' It would be entirely out of consideration to realize your loved one had died and that you can hear from TMZ.' A joint press conference describing the collision's early details took place at 2:30 p.m., the Los Angeles County Sheriff & Los Angeles County Fire Department. Los Angeles County Fire Chief Daryl Osby announced that the Federal Aviation Administration had been reviewing and the National Transport Safety Board (NTSB). A "Go Team" of 18 people, including NTSB investigators and specialists, came at night to find a flight recorder. As a consequence of the accident, an inquiry into Lockheed Martin's Sikorsky S-76B was conducted. Sheriff Villanueva advised people to stay away because people flooded the crashed field, and traffic was disrupted. The FAA placed a five-mile no-flight zone up to 5000 feet around the crash site. On the first evening after the crash, the medical testator-coroner removed the remains of three of the nine victims overnight.[41] Sheriff Villanueva appointed members to patrol the rough terrain on horseback and on all-terrain vehicles to enforce a secure perimeter and prevent access by hunters of souvenirs.

The next day the pilot was confirmed to be "too weak for flight follow," which he asked for, just before the helicopter plummeted into the hillside by air traffic controllers. This indicates that the aircraft was too far to be controlled by air traffic control, but it was not too far to fly safely.

On 28 January, the Medical Examiner-Coroner had retrieved all nine remains from the crash site. On 28 January, the remains of Kobe Bryant and three others were fingerprinted, and the other five bodies were found on 30 January after the identification and review of DNA. Autopsies took place on 28 January. On February 1, most of the victims ' remains, including Bryants, were issued to their relatives by the Medical Examiner-Coroner.

On 31 January, a spokesman of the National Transport Safety Board said that Island Express Helicopters, which operated the crashed aircraft, were not licensed to operate in foggy weather; whether the pilot-operated on instruments at the time of the crash is unclear.

Authorities moved the remains of the aircraft from Los Angeles to Phoenix, Arizona, on 30 January. Nevertheless, the safe perimeter persisted around the crash site, awaiting removal by a private hazmat clean-up crew under the California Toxic Material Control Department of dangerous materials (mainly fuel and hydraulic fluids).

The NTSB issued an "inquiry report" on the accident on February 7. Final results, reasons, and suggestions will not be anticipated until the full report 12-18 months after the NTSB releases the incident. Preliminary findings from the NTSB assessment show no evidence of engine failure. The report says that... the viewable parts of engines showed no signs of uncontained or disastrous internal loss and that the harm to the blades "was compatible at impact with controlled rotation." The damage and ensuing fire "highly fragmented" many aircraft, engine, cockpit, and instrumentation were.

Memorials

About 200 gathered at the bottom of the hill near the crash, many with Bryant's jersey and basketball. People had created an unofficial gathering at the Staples Center, the home arena for the Los Angeles Lakers (the organization that Bryant operated with) just hours before the Grammy Awards were scheduled. The concert was highlighted by "It is so hard to say goodbye to yesterday" presented by Alicia Keys and Boyz II Men, who celebrated Bryant with other artists such as Lil Nas X, Lizzo, Ru-DMC, Aerosmith, and DJ Khaled. Bryant's two retired jerseys in the Staples Center rafters were illuminated by the sun. The employees at Staples Center started clearing out of the arena the renovation wall; however, they vowed to gather, pack and ship all the non-perishable products to their families a week after Bryant's passing. The items found included 1,350 basketballs, 25,000 cards and notes, five thousand signs or messages, five hundred plush Animaux, three hundred pairs of shoes, and fourteen banners.' Supporters built a Bryant monument outside of the Kobe Bryant Gymnasium in Ardmore, Pennsylvania, attended by Bryant from 1992 to 1996. Jerseys, basketballs, teddy bears, roses, and torches, all of them have been brought together to honor Bryant.

Bryant's brilliant purple and gold photos become icons nationwide, including the Los Angeles International Airport, the Madison Square Garden, the Empire State Building, and Santa Ana Water Tower in Orange County, California.

On February 2, pictures of Kobe Bryant and his girlfriend Gianna appeared on the world's highest landmark, Burj Khalifa. The show was coordinated by Ahmed Sultan Bin Sulayem, Executive Chairman of the Dubai Multi Commodities Center (DMCC).

On the 7th of February, Kobe and Gianna Bryant were reunited at the Pacific View Memorial Park's private cemetery in Newport Beach's Corona del Mar community. Until then, the most successful resident of the tiny graveyard was John Wayne.

NBA Commissioner Adam Silver said in a statement:

The NBA fraternity is shocked by Kobe Bryant's horrific death and Gianna's daughter... Over 20 seasons,

Kobe taught us what it means to merge remarkable talent and utter commitment to success. He was one of the most extraordinary players in our game's history with legendary achievements... But he is most known for encouraging people worldwide to take a basketball and play to their very highest. He was generous with the expertise he acquired and saw it as his goal to share it with future generations of players, loving Gianna, particularly in his love of the game.

Initially too busy to speak to the media, Gregg Downer, Bryant's high school basketball mentor, was "completely shocked and saddened." Downer trained Bryant at Lower Merion High School in western Philadelphia from 1992 to 1996 and captured the 1996 Bryant State Championship.

With whom Bryant has been frequently compared, Michael Jordan said in a statement, "Words can not describe the sadness I felt. I loved Kobe–he was like a little brother to me... We talked a lot often and those talks I will miss very much. He was a formidable competitor, one of the great men and a creative force." Kareem Abdul-Jabbar shared his condolences on Facebook. LeBron James, who had placed Bryant on the NBA career scoring leader's chart last night and had spoken to Bryant on the Morning of the crash on Twitter, wrote, "I am sad and saddened... I assure you that I will continue your legacy." Jerry West, Laker's grand and general manager who negotiated

Bryant's transfer deal for the Lakers, added, "I do not believe you can start your legacy."

Owner Dallas Mavericks Mark Cuban says "that the Dallas Maverick's Number 24 will never again be worn." Several previously uniformed NBA players decided to switch to new numbers in honor of Bryant.

Gianna was a supporter of the women's UConn Huskies basketball team and played in several tournaments, and had wanted to go to university to compete. UConn posted a jersey picture and flowers with the dedication post' A Husky forever.'

Three days after the accident, the NBA canceled Los Angeles Lakers' clash with Los Angeles Clippers set for 28 January. On January 30th, the first game between the Clippers and Kings after the crash, the Clippers honored Bryant before the game, and Paul George told Bryant about a video tribute. The next day after the accident against the Portland Trail Blazers, the Lakers played their first game. In anticipation of the match, Lakers paid a salute to Bryant and all the people who lost their lives in an incident at a ceremony held shortly before the end, with Usher performing the National Anthem "Amazing Grace" and Boyz II Men, while Wiz Khalifa and Charlie Puth assembled at half-time to perform "See again." James also delivered a speech before the game to the fans, and Bryant's name was revealed for every player in the Lakers launch. The game was ESPN's second most-watched game, with 4,41 million viewers on average.

On 5 February 2020, Gianna's Harbor Day School removed her number 2 uniform.

Commissioner Adam Silver revealed on February 15 that the NBA All-Star Game MVP Award would now be revamped into the NBA All-Star Game Kobe Bryant's Most Valuable Player, presented by Bryant. Moreover, each player on Team Giannis wears the 24th uniform, at Team LeBron 2020, in memory of his daughter.

Other sports

Many players, teams, and other organizations in the Major League, National Football League and National Hockey League commemorated Bryant immediately after the crash.

In the 2020 Pro Bowl, several athletes paid their respects during condolences and celebratory tributes to Bryant. The Chiefs in Kansas City and San Francisco 49ers gathered on the 24-yard line on their respective sides and kept a moment of silence at Super Bowl LIV to mourn the collision involving Bryant, his family, and the other seven victims, along with Chris Doleman, who passed away two days after Bryant. The venue Super Bowl LIV, Hard Rock Stadium, was also lit up in the colors of Bryant's purple and gold lakers the day after the accident.

In its 2020 Royal Rumble Pay-per-View, WWE paid tribute to Bryant later that night, as did All Elite Wrestling at AEW Dynamite throughout Cleveland during this week of SoCal Uncensored group from Southern California with Bryant jerseys and many professional wrestlers shared their condolence for the Bryant fans.

During the 2020 Australian Open, several Tour Tennis players, including Novak Djokovic, paid tribute to Bryant, who noted that "I was one of the best athletes of all time— he influenced me, and so many other people all over the world." A.C. Milan, Bryant's favorite team, was growing up and wore black armbands that remember him in their match against Turino at Coppa Italia on 28 January, while there was also a minute of silence before the game. During tournaments and social media, numerous soccer players and teams paid tribute to Bryant. On 26 January 2020, after scoring his second goal against Lille OSC from the punishment point, Neymar paid Bryant tribute, hitting four fingers from his right hand and two fingers from his left hand to mark the number 24 camera praying to heaven.

U.S. President Donald Trump, previous US President Bill Clinton and former U.S. President Barack Obama Secretary of State Hillary Clinton, Governor Gavin Newsom of California, Mayor Eric Garcetti of Los Angeles, and other Americans politicians have condolen.

"We're utterly devastated by the sudden loss of my adoring husband, Kobe — the incredible father of our babies, and my beautiful, gentle Gianna— Natalia, Bianka, and Capri's caring, compassionate and wonderful daughter, and wonderful friend," Bryant's Vanessa posted on Instagram. "There aren't enough terms right now to express our sorrow. I find comfort in the knowledge that Kobe and Gigi understood that both were so deeply loved. We were so incredibly blessed to have them in our lives. They were here with us forever.

The Black mamba mentality Analysis and more

The influence of Kobe Bryant remains keen on people all over the world. Since the news broke from the early death of the former basketball star, people have tried to express their emotions and what Bryant means to them.

It requires just one swipe across any social media platform to see that Bryant has inspired people from all over the planet by his acts on and off the field. Although Bryant's heritage is controlled by some bad decisions and situations, including his 2003 case of sexual assault, there is one thing that everyone can agree on: his mentality of Mamba.

How Kobe Bryant crafted the Mamba mentality

Kobe Bryant's loyalty to basketball can not be summed up in one account, but there is a small incident near to doing justice. Indeed, it was not one of the countless prominent accomplishments of his 20-season NBA career. Alternatively, in a picture, a few months before he died in a helicopter accident on Sunday, he shared on his Instagram.

Bryant posted an image of himself posing by his youth basketball squad from the Mamba Sports Academy. All around the middle school level, the kids look effortlessly when carrying cups that have marked the fourth place for them. Once Bryant first posted the picture that dated back two years ago, he added: "the 7th participant (not pictured) skipped this dance recital so it could tell you where it's in focus right now." As Giri Nathan of Deadspin noted, Bryant found that he had to change his remarks to justify himself slightly better and added: "I think that she'd like it." Now? Now? She consumes food and breathes the game. "There's a tragic postscript for the photo, realizing what we currently do, that both Bryant and his father will lose their lives on their way to the Mamba Sports Academy. However, when Bryant posted it, it made the social media rounds a humorous remembrance of his passion for the sport. This would have been an opening, with any other famous athlete, for simple goodwill: here was this living legend who, under his new youth coaching system, earned five NBA titles and two Olympic gold medals. Instead, it was an indication that he took to his new position the same attitude he won titles with the Lakers. If you were a player in the Hall of Fame or a teenage dance lover doesn't matter, Bryant would ask you the most.

He named the mindset of Mamba and even wrote a book about it. "I liked to challenge people and make them unpleasant," he wrote in a Players ' Tribune excerpt. "It contributes to introspection, and this leads to change. It was not a quality that leads himself to a popularity contest; he was a notoriously tricky team-mate during his years as a footballer. Phil Jackson, his former head coach, once wrote a book in which he found Bryant "uncoachable." Bryant didn't argue the point correctly.

He was phenomenally successful, though, as he made his enemies much worse as he told you when you were on the same team. Bryant would be the first to admit that he took the NBA player of his generation after Michael Jordan. He took the legendary competitive nature of Jordan to his logical endpoint in his style of playing. While Jordan masked his sociopathic approach to the game behind a flat, brilliant person created by Madison Avenue, Bryant followed the opposite path and played it, becoming practically guided by the boos. If you called yourself after a poisonous snake, you knew you wouldn't be Warner Bros ' friendly protagonist. Bryant wrote in the Mamba Mentality, "I also tried to kill the opponent.

Let's not ignore that he first obtained the Black Mamba name. As Kent Babb of the Washington Post paraphrased a fascinating report on the shooting guard, Bryant believed that the position "was the only way that he could step past Colorado's events." Ironically, such "idents" culminated in a sexual assault charge in 2003 and a subsequent trial. After the accuser refused to testify and a civil action was later settled off the court, the criminal case was dismissed. After the fact, Bryant's own words rejected: "I now understand how she feels she did not agree to the meeting."

Robert Silverman of the Daily Beast has claimed firmly that Bryant used the idea that a large segment of the population felt he was a murderer as his drive-in sentencing. In an all too common sports tale, a story that began as one of violence against women was slowly turned into a narrative about a competitor who overcomes adversity.

In the end, Bryant's tactic paid off. During the rest of his career, Bryant became willing to be a one-person wrecking crew, a bucket terminator configured. Bryant recorded 81 points in a 2006 match against the Toronto Raptors, the second-highest total in the NBA history. It was this Bryant who won his last two titles without Shaq's big shadow. As the League grew more concerned with shot efficacy towards the end of his career, Bryant also angrily protested against the day's shifting philosophy. His big shooting nights were popular, and he took and often fired low-value shots at a pace almost unacceptable to basic mathematics. It was apt that he recorded 60 points for an outstanding 50 shot attempt in his last NBA game.

It would have been absurd for a lesser player to try, but Bryant was so incredible that it didn't matter. Indeed, he was the all-time leader of missed shots and the fourth in the all-time leaderboard. A day before his death, LeBron James, currently with the Lakers himself, placed him on the list. The success of James eventually became the focus of Bryant's last tweet.

''Continuing to move the game forward @KingJames. Much respect to my brother #33644.''

So, what exactly is Mamba mentality?

What is the mamba mentality?

For Bryant, mamba mentality was about more than just basketball.

" Mamba mentality is everything about focusing on the process and trusting in the effort when it matters most," he told Amazon Book Review. "It's the ultimate mantra for the competitive spirit. It started simply as a hashtag that came to me one day, and it's become something professional athletes -- and even non-athletes-- embrace as a state of mind."

" Hard work outweighs talent-- every time," he continued. "Mamba mentality is about 4 a.m. exercises, doing more than the next man and then relying on in the work you've put in when it's time to perform.

The mindset became such a phenomenon that Bryant wrote a book about it.

Bryant talked about the mindset and how he passed it on to other gamers, like Lebron James.

" I always intended to eliminate the opposition," he wrote. "The main point LeBron and I went over were what constitutes a killer mentality. He watched how I approached every single practice, and I continuously challenged him and the rest of the people. When we were messing around; I keep in mind there was one half. I entered the locker room at half-time and asked the guys-- in a less PG way-- what in the hell we were doing. In the second half, LeBron responded in a huge method. He brought out a dominant state of mind. And I've seen him lead that way since."

The mamba movement has influenced more than just professional athletes. Fans everywhere are now utilizing the expression as inspiration to keep going, keep pressing, and keep battling.

The alter-ego helped Bryant cultivate his philosophy. Just mentioned, Mamba mentality means "simply trying to improve every day." It's the "easiest type of simply attempting to get much better at whatever you're doing."

Sure, it's not mind-blowing as far as viewpoint goes; however, it is useful and actionable.

In his Mamba Mentality autobiography, Bryant discusses the significance of proficiency and the lessons of failure in more detail. He discusses the power of fascination:

If you desire to be fantastic in a specific location, you need to consume it. Many individuals say they want to be excellent, but they're not prepared to make the sacrifices essential to success. They have other concerns, whether crucial or not, and they spread themselves out.

It's simple for individuals to point at masters like Bryant and remark that their talent is simply God-given. The truth is that even though some might have natural attributes or capabilities, what identifies the common from the extraordinary is the quantity of work and dedication put into refining a craft. Bryant understood this most excellent.

Bryant was always the first to show up at practice, in some cases injured, and often before the lights even came on-- sometimes five hours before training also started. As soon as heated up before practice from 4:15 a.m. to 11 a.m., he declined to leave up until he made 800 shots.

Even in high school, Bryant would practice from 5 a.m. until 7 a.m.-- before classes began. He would also challenge his high school colleagues to individual matches, initially to 100. He won his worst video game 100-12.

Off the court, Bryant was simply as compulsive. He cold-called and texted numerous company individuals and entrepreneurs to select their brains about success, sometimes at 3 a.m. He started his own media business dedicated to storytelling and produced a short animated documentary that won an Oscar. He taught himself to play Beethoven's "Moonlight Sonata" by ear on the piano.

There's no rejecting Bryant was hyper-focused in his pursuit of greatness. How much of that can be credited to "natural ability"?

In addition to proficiency, one should accept failure as part of a reasonable procedure. Failure is inescapable, and when gone about the proper way, it has a lot to teach us about enhancement. On the importance of it, Bryant states:

If I desired to implement something brand-new into my game, I'd see it and try including it right away. I wasn't scared of missing, looking bad, or being humiliated. That's because I always kept the result, the extended video game, in my mind. I continually focused on the fact that I had to attempt something to get it, and once I got it, I'd have another tool in my toolbox. I was OK with that if the rate was a lot of work and a couple of missed out on shots.

"Mamba mentality is a constant quest to discover responses. It's that keen interest to wish to be much better, to figure things out. Mamba mentality is you're going; you're competing, you're not stressed over completion result.

You're not stressed about any of that; you're focused on being in the minute. That's what mamba mentality is," Kobe describes.

Bryant recognized that if you wish to enhance or learn something new, you're going to fail at your very first attempts. Through repetition and trials, you will eventually improve. When you comprehend that, failure becomes an essential tool in improving yourself.

That's an essential thing to bear in mind. What inhibits many from achieving and even pursuing goals is the fear of failure or humiliating oneself.

Fellow G.O.A.T. Michael Jordan puts it this way:

During my lifetime, I took more than 9,000 shots. I lost nearly 300 tournaments. I have been expected to take the winning shot and missed twenty-six occasions. In my life, I've failed over and over and over again. And that's why I'm good.

It was an endless cycle.

ESPN sports analyst Jay Williams, retired NBA player, shared a story one day when he was ready to face the Lakers.

Until 7 p.m. Williams opted to hit the Staples Center at 3 p.m. tip-off. Put some extra effort into it. Kobe was already working out and incomplete contact when he entered. Williams went through his training and called it quits after approximately an hour.

Kobe didn't.

Mamba invested another 25 minutes on the floor before he struck the showers. He scored 40 points that night.

Williams asked after the game why Kobe remained out there so long.

" Because I saw you walk in."

The unrelenting effort to pursue success will be Kobe's everlasting impact on the world. Sure, he was among the most decorated professional athletes to stroll the earth; however, that can't be passed on.

Hundreds and thousands of athletes have embraced the Mamba Mentality and others around the world. She put in the work to be one of the finest young basketball gamers in the nation, pursuing her dream of one day becoming a Husky.

If you made it this far, I implore you to embrace the mindset of the Mamba. No matter who you are, where you're from or what you do, makes every effort much better. Work every day to be the finest you can be. Awaken early. Go to sleep late. Do what it takes to achieve achievement.

That's how the Mamba lived.

Mamba mentality utilization in Your Own Life

Bryant expressed his Mamba mindset in the expectation of bringing their success to numerous individuals, teams, and organizations. You don't have to be a superstar to refresh this philosophy in your own life.

Think of what Bryant was trying to convey. May things might you refer to in your life? Are you good at certain things that you could become a master of? Are you doing the work you need to master? Would you cause fear of failure to hinder your productive pursuit?

Bryant acknowledged the impact of the representatives. Will Durant (summing up Aristotle) said in these words, "We are what we continuously do. Excellence, then, is not an event but a practice. "Bryant has been ripped out of this so young country; it is heartbreaking. Nonetheless, one of the best ways to honor the dead is to make the best of their character and bring it into your existence so that the glory of the departed shines in you.

This can be the right way to see the future of a leader. Even after we quit this body, this is the effect on others. While Bryant is gone, his reputation remains defined by his commitment to excellence.

Steps to practicing a mamba mentality

Some of our motivating readers on Monday might say, "I'm not an athlete, and I don't even like basketball." Nonetheless, I will say that some of you are reading this are company owners, executives, kids, and people who work hard to improve things, develop things, and live well. For each of you, Kobe had letters. And all of us. He encouraged all of us to be better athletes, better leaders, and better people.

"To concentrate on the cycle and support the hard work is the mindset of Mamba," and "the ultimate slogan for the competitive spirit. While most see Mamba as something unique to athletes, the fact is that we can all compete in the game of life by embracing the Mamba. Below are the components of this slogan that guarantee positive results.

1. Difficult Work

An effort will always produce excellent outcomes with time. Kobe believed that "hard work outweighs skill." There is no denying the truth that you will come across people who present in specific locations surpass yours in life. However, the effort can intensify how your presents are gotten because your efficiency will promote you.

2. Self-confidence and don't be afraid to stop working

Your tough work needs to be coupled with confidence continuously. You ought to believe in yourself and what your difficult task will produce in spite of. Since Kobe entered the league, fresh out of high school, he was implicated of being cocky. I like to call Kobe's mindset self-confidence; however, either method, he thought in himself. Kobe's confidence allowed him to move without hesitation; it also daunted less favorable challengers. While Kobe was often compared to greats that came before him, he believed in himself so much so that he only wished to be the most beautiful variation of Kobe Bryant he could be. When compared to basketball excellent Michael Jordan, Kobe confidently stated, "I do not want to be the next Michael Jordan, I only want to be Kobe Bryant" Understand, Confidence is key, and thinking straight impacts what you attain because success requires a specific level of boldness.

Failure isn't a subject that people typically like to discuss, specifically in Monday inspiration columns. It's awkward. Awkward. And the majority of us don't wish to air our failures openly. Mega-stars like Kobe had their failures publicized from every miss on the court that we enjoyed life to all the bits in the tabloids. Everybody fails. Even legends. Those who learn from their failures and use those lessons learned are the ones who go on to be effective.

" I've practiced and practiced and played numerous times. There's absolutely nothing truly to be scared of when you think about it. I've failed in the past, and I awakened the next early morning, and I'm OK. Once you understand what failure seems like, determination goes after success." ~ Kobe Bryant.

3. follow your heart

Just about every entrepreneur-- active and stopped working-- has said that you need to pursue what you are passionate about. Making it through the great days is severe enough; if you're not inspired by what you're doing, you'll never survive the bad days. Follow your heart. Consider it only briefly unattainable if it appears unattainable. Assembled a step-wise plan that will get you on the course to your passion.

" You do not wish to jump into something if you're not passionate about it." ~ Kobe Bryant

4. increase up, don't let frustration bring you down

You've stopped working, or you're floundering. The longer that you've been spinning, the harder it is to untether yourself from all that has dissuaded you so that you can prepare to rise. Ultimately, you reach a point where you recognize that you need to break free from what's holding you back.

Tackle it one step at a time. Right. Left. Left. Put one foot in front of the other. Monday's motivation is everything about additive and incremental progress. "Overnight success" is anything. Do one thing, then the next. One, two. One, two. Just GO FOR IT!

Day by day, one day at a time. No one dislikes the great ones. ~ Kobe Bryant

5. Eliminate Everything

The name "Black Mamba" was born from Quentin Tarantino's Kill Bill. In the film, the mamba snake described deadly assassins; according to Kobe, his goal was always to "to kill the opposition." Not an actual death but one that eliminates the competitions while raising the bar. This kills whatever mindset leaves no room for anything other than success. No matter the video game, a control state of mind is crucial to winning. You should murder whatever that stands between you and a victory. It's either be or kill killed, and I'm favorable you didn't begin your journey to take an L.

He not just pressed himself on a ruthless path to perfection to "leave the game a legend" however set himself up-- and others-- for their success. In reality, his second chapter as a #girldad promoting athleticism and equality may ultimately prove to be his greatest. No doubt, his tradition will likely extend off the hardwood court and survive on well beyond his untimely death.

"The essential thing is to try and motivate individuals so that they can be great at whatever they want to do." ~ Kobe Bryant

A practical explanation of mamba mentality (Kobe Bryant)

I remember when, as a kid, I got my first real basketball.

I loved the feel of it in my hands. I was so enamored with the ball that I didn't

wish to bounce it or utilize it since I didn't want to mess up the pebbled leather grains or

the perfect grooves. I didn't want to ruin the feel.

I enjoyed the sound of it, too. The tap, tap, tap of when a ball bounces on the wood.

The clarity and clarity. The predictability. The noise of life and light.

Those are some of the components that I liked about the ball about the game. They were at

the core and root of my process and craft. They were the reasons I went through all that I went through, put in all that I put in, dug as deep as I dug.

It all returned to that special tap, tap, tap that I initially grew fixated with as a kid.

My balance, as a young player, is off.

Look at the dichotomy between us, starting with posture. Michael is standing directly from the waist up. He's not leaning in either instruction and because of that, he is balanced and focused. He is in control of his body and the play.

Compare all that to my defense. Now, I'm using my forearm to thrust weight into his back, similar to they teach it. Unfortunately, that's about all I'm doing right. I'm leaning forward, which is a significant no-no, and putting excessive pressure on him. That alone, by dint of gravity, triggers me to be off-balance. As an outcome, one relocation by Michael, one absolute spin right or feint left, would throw me off and give him space to either shoot or spin-off of me. This defense is no Bueno.

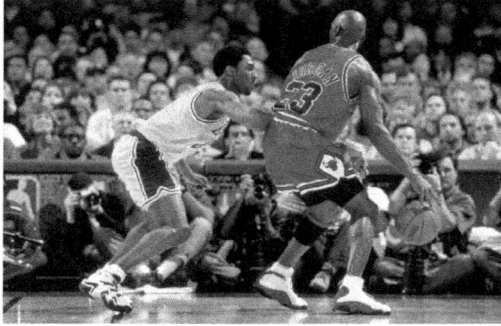

Luckily, I saw this shot in 1998. I changed my stance and equilibrium after observing it. It was much easier to work against me in the article afterward.

Allen Iverson was little, but he was incredible too.

My strategy was to take advantage of my height and aim over it. I don't have to do anything; I don't have to go anywhere, I don't have to fight to get him. I'm just going to shoot at him because I can get a clean look.

What I'm thinking about isn't the same as a sweater. I often received the ball in desirable positions while Allen protected me, targeting areas like the middle wall because he couldn't deter me from catching a pass.

But maybe in the post, I couldn't have identified it even closer? Should I not take him away from the dribble at 25 feet? Perhaps, but that wouldn't have been wise.

I did not pick the ball in the post because the Sixers would just have cut me off and caught me. I could have squared and dribbled, but they would also have supported and stuck in this case. I mitigate all these plans by capturing it on the elbow and the mid-wing because they could not lead me on the pass, and I didn't have to dribble to get an open look over it.

Over the years, I wouldn't say my leadership style improved.

I enjoyed confronting and awkward men. This leads to introspection, and it leads to improvement. You may argue that I dared to make people their brightest.

This strategy has never fluctuated. Nonetheless, what I changed was how I varied from player to player. I always questioned all of them and left them nervous; I just showed it to them. To learn what would fit and for whom, I began doing research and looking at what they were doing. I knew their tales and witnessed their aspirations. I learned what made them feel secure and their most significant doubts. If I had it, I would make the most of it by hitting the right nerve at the right time.

I've always been trying to kill the opposition. LeBron and I spoke about what makes a killer spirit. He saw how I treated through action and ever confronted him and the others.

I recall when we played around, there was a fifth. I returned to the locker room at half time and asked the guys — less in PG fashion— what we do in the hole. In the second half, LeBron reacted much— he came out with a genuinely dominant attitude. And since then, I've seen him lead the direction.

Obsession Is Natural to me

On November 12, 1996, Allen Iverson dropped 35 on the Knicks in a win at the Garden.

On November 12, 1996, I played 5 minutes and completed two points in a Lakers win at Houston.

I lost it when I inspected my hotel room later that night and saw the 35 at the SportsCenter. I turned the table, tossed the chairs, broke the TV.

I thought I had been working hard.

5 minutes. Two points.

I needed to work more difficult.

I did.

On March 19, 1999, Iverson put 41 points and ten helps on me in Philadelphia.

Working harder wasn't enough.

I had to study this guy maniacally.

I obsessively checked out every article and book I could discover about AI. I fanatically viewed every game he had played, returning to the IUPU All-American Game. I fanatically studied his every success and his every struggle. I fanatically looked for any weak point I might discover.

I searched the world for musings to contribute to my AI Musecage.

This led me to study how great white sharks hunt seal the coast of South Africa.

Persistence. The timing. The angles.

On Feb 20, 2000, in Philadelphia, PJ gave me the task of guarding AI at the start of the second half. No one knew how much this difficulty suggested to me

I desired him to feel the disappointment I felt.

I wanted everyone who laughed at the 41 and 10 he put on me to choke on their laughter.

He would openly say that neither of us might stop the other.

I declined to believe that.

I score 50.

You score absolutely no.

THAT is what I think.

When I began safeguarding AI, he had 16 at the half. He ended up the game with 16.

Vengeance was sweet.

I wasn't satisfied after the win. I was irritated that he had made me feel that method in the first place.

I swore, from that point on, to approach every matchup as a matter of life and death. No one was going to have that type of control over my focus ever once again.

I will choose who I want to target and lock-in.

I will select whether your objectives for the upcoming season compromise where I desire to be 20 years.

Suppose they do not, happy hunting to you. However, if they do ... I will hunt you fanatically. It's just natural to me.

Lessons From Kobe Bryant

The world of business has started to become more dynamic. It is essential to note that the same competition, which led Kobe to a great deal, will win other victories which small and large corporations can and should accept.

On the other side, a company is more than rivalry, and achievement requires skill, motivation, and dedication. Kobe Bryant had all these qualities in spades, and throughout his illustrious career, he showed them.

Kobe Bryant also had a great passion for the game, which was evident in his superior hardwood play. Regardless of the field in which you are, you must be enthusiastic about what you are doing as a business owner.

The same attitude that brought him to performance Spring's success in your company over and over again.

Everyone who wants to sell can quickly understand Mamba's values as to business psychology. Mamba Mentality principles are dynamic. They transcend the sports world as they should apply to corporate psychology and marketing.

Whether it is channeled into athletics or marketing, victory is assured when you embrace Mamba Mentality.

Let's look at what the individual of Black Mamba implied to Kobe Bryant and how this is associated with the company before discussing some of the most significant maxims of the Mamba mindset.

The Black Mamba has been created by Kobe Bryant to distinguish his work from his private life. The person helped him in innumerable ways. It helped him to release his challenges and focus every time he went on the hardwood on his professional performance.

Anyone in industry or promotion will profit from the emphasis he has put on his Black Mamba alter ego. It reminds us to leave our problems at the door and give everything to us when we work. While we all have issues in our personal lives, we will stop impacting our workforce's efficiency and profitability.

Another message to take into consideration in any vital business choice in Kobe Bryant's brilliantly succinct Mamba Mentality; he clarified that it's about putting away one's apprehension of what people can say or if they are upset and concentrating on being at the moment.

Such terms have a particularly profound impact on businesspeople in today's politically charged and volatile environment. You can travel too gradually and lose momentum because you spend too much time and energy thinking about who, what, and how an ad or business decision would upset the public. Concentrate on the moment, take the time, be the moment, and fuck with all other stuff. This is Mamba Mentality in brief, and it would be beneficial for businesses to implement it if they were to surmount the rivalry.

You must be strategic in this business and act quickly, but you must be brave above all. If you want to win, you have to hit on the hardwood like Black Mamba.

The Mamba Mentality and What it Means for Marketing Psychology

The Mamba Mentality was another magnificent gift Kobe Bryant left us. The same attitude that brought him over and over again to triumph can be used to carry your business success.

Anyone with a business bent can understand Mamba's beliefs of consumer science readily. Mamba Mentality principles are dynamic. They surpass the sporting world as they can quickly be extended to corporate psychology and promotion.

Whether you're channeled through sports or publicity, success is expected as you take up the Mamba Mentality.

Until discussing some of the essential Mamba Mentality maxims, let's talk about what the Black Mamba person meant for Kobe Bryant.

Kobe Bryant developed the Black Mamba to distinguish his professional life from his personal life. The person helped him in innumerable ways. It allowed him to release his challenges and concentrate every time he entered the rugged forest on his professional performance.

Anyone in industry or promotion will take advantage of the emphasis he used to adopt his Black Mamba's alter ego. This reminds us to put our troubles at the door and give everything to us as we come to work. While we all have personal challenges, we must avoid such problems from impacting organizational efficiency and profitability.

Kobe Bryant's perfectly concise description of Mamba Mentality offers another message to carry to heart in any critical business move. He clarified that it's about tossing away the fear of what people might say or if they're upset and are focused on being correct now.

Such terms have a particularly profound impact on businesspeople in today's politically charged and highly sensitive environment. You will be too late and lose momentum because you spend too much time and effort thinking about who and how an event or business action would offend people. Concentrate on the moment, take a moment, be the moment, and fuck with everything else. That's Mamba Mentality, and if companies want to rise above the competition, they will do well to embrace it.

In this environment, you must be strategic to act quickly, but you must be brave above all. If you want the business to succeed, you have to strike on the hardwood like the Black Mamba.

Kobe Bryant Quotes to Make Your Business, a Winner

Although he referred to sport in the following quotations, companies can channel their knowledge into the roof to drive performance. Here are some of the Kobe Bryant quotations that are most motivational and relevant.

"I don't want to be Kobe Bryant the next Michael Jordan. As a product, you could imagine more prominent companies, but that is an error. You don't want to be like the company down the street; it's crucial to create your unique brand, which has meaning for itself on the menu.

"Winning takes absolute precedence—a grey area. There is no grey area. This should be taken to heart by every decision-maker in business. The competitive spirit is fundamental to any productive company. You must go to the throat and play to win or not.

"If you're afraid to fail, possibly you should struggle." Those phrases have to be taken to heart by the company. The global marketplace is no position for shyness; you must focus on your products and services. If you do not like what you sell, why should the consumer? Why should the consumer?

"I learned that intimidation doesn't happen when you're in the right frame of mind." Kobe Bryant fits well with the previous quote because it shows us we don't need to be threatened by rivals or the lack of ourselves with the right mentality. The right mentality is a trusting one with the foresight and courage to succeed.

"If you realize what the loss is, persistence pursues achievement." Kobe's words reassure us here that it should strengthen our appetite for excellence instead of serving as a dissuasive tool if we lose. If you let down a loss, you're going to stay down. Come back on this horse to try to do better, the attitude, the mamba mentality, all.

"Everything that is negative-pressure challenges-is a chance for me to rise." Maybe this is one of Kobe Bryant's most useful maxims.

CONCLUSION

Although the loss of Kobe Bryant has saddened all of us, his achievements and his words live on; if there's one thing we know about the magnificent Black Mamba, it's that he would not want any of us to be disheartened for long. He would want us to get our heads back in the game and push more difficult than ever to succeed.

Here are a few of his most informative and inspiring quotes.

" If it's a bear and me, with the bear." Kobe Bryant

" Haters are an excellent problem to have. Nobody hates the good ones. They dislike the terrific ones."

Kobe Bryant

" Great things originate from tough work and determination. No Excuses." Kobe Bryant

" I'm reflective only in the sense that I discover to progress. I reflect with a function." Kobe Bryant

We leave you with this final quote, a Kobe-ism that represents the legendary Black Mamba himself.

" I'm chasing perfection." Kobe Bryant

When said, Kobe said, "The most crucial thing is to attempt and motivate individuals so that they can be great at whatever they desire to do." In his usual style, he achieved success in that pursuit.

The legacy of Kobe "Bean" Bryant, in addition to the memories of his 13-year-old daughter, Gianna, and the other seven passengers who died together in the crash.

Mamba Mentality touched the hearts of millions of individuals all over the world, and in the NBA, gamers benefited considerably by using it to their game. In June 2016, when Cleveland Cavaliers won their first NBA title, their point guard Kyrie Irving told the reporters after the game, "That moment right there occurred, and I resembled 'okay, I'm fine. And all I was thinking of in the back of my mind was Mamba mentality. Just Mamba mentality, that's all I was believing."

MAMBA OUT

DISCLAIMER

This book was written by a passionate Lakers fan who wanted to create something beautiful in honor of his idol!

It's not an official book.

This book is not intended as a substitute for the medical advice of physicians. The reader should regularly consult a physician in matters relating to his/her health, particularly concerning any symptoms requiring diagnosis or medical attention.

Do Not Go Yet; One Last Thing To Do

If you enjoyed this book or found it useful, I'd be very grateful if you'd post a short review on Amazon. Your support does make a difference, and I read all the reviews personally to get your feedback and make this book even better.

Thanks again for your support!

CPSIA information can be obtained
at www.ICGtesting.com
Printed in the USA
LVHW081522221221
706945LV00016B/221

9 781914 038334